June 2009

Building Information Exchange for First Responders Workshop: Proceedings

October 15-16, 2008

Jason D. Averill, David Holmberg, Alan Vinh, and William Davis

Abstract

Presently, there is no integrated solution for delivering building data into the hands of emergency responders. Technically, there are many challenges to collect, format, process, integrate and transport building data out of the building. Beyond this, the system for making building data available must mesh with public safety networks and dispatch and emergency responder interface requirements, securely and reliably. While many stakeholder industries are working on individual technical issues, this workshop will help to ensure that the entire process has an efficient and reliable flow.

The workshop on Building Information Exchange for First Responders on October 15-16, 2008 brought together key stakeholders in a dialogue on the delivery of building information to the first responder communities in order to identify opportunities for collaboration and standardization.

Primary topics include the PSAP network interface, communication protocols, data encapsulation standards, and security (including user and machine authentication and verification).

Table of Contents

Introduction

Today, when first responders arrive at a building in response to an emergency they typically have very little information about what is happening beyond a high-level summary (such as, a fire has been reported, a break in has occurred, there is a medical emergency, etc) or limited information from callers to emergency services which may be incorrect, outdated, or incomplete. As a result, valuable time must be spent determining the nature of the emergency and details of the building and its systems that are relevant to a response, and the number and type of emergency personnel who may be needed to carry out an effective response. For fire emergencies, risks to building occupants and firefighters escalate exponentially with time; therefore, timely on-scene assessment and faster situation awareness will improve the event outcomes for lives and property.

Modern building automation systems increasingly involve integration of HVAC, fire, access control and other systems that contain a wealth of sensor data and other information that could potentially be helpful to first responders. Industry has begun to recognize this potential and document the information needs of first responders. Development of products that can provide this information quickly, reliably, and in a usable form is inhibited by a lack of enabling measurement science (i.e., standard data models, communication protocols, user interface standards, security procedures, and testing tools).

Objectives and Participants

The objective of the meeting was to bring together key stakeholders in order to discuss how to deliver building information to the first responder communities and identify opportunities for collaboration and standardization. The individual participants are indicated below in Table 1. The participants represent a cross-section of academic, industry, and local and federal government stakeholders.

Jason D. Averill **NIST** **100 Bureau Dr** **Gaithersburg, MD 20899-8664** **Phone:** (301) 975-2585 **Fax:** (301) 975-4052 **E-mail:** jason.averill@nist.gov **Web Page:** www.bfrl.nist.gov	**David M. Coggeshall** **Managing Director** **San Francisco Communications** **79 Rossi Avenue** **San Francisco, CA 94118** **Phone:** (415) 387-8760 **E-mail:** IBComm@AOL.com **Web Page:** maplab.org

Toby Considine
Consultant
Phone: 9196192104
E-mail: toby.considine@gmail.com

Diegane (DiDi) Dione
Founder & Chief Innovation Officer
Dione Systems
Six MetroTech Center
Brooklyn, NY 11201
Phone: (718) 260-3926
Mobile: (602) 432-8711
E-mail:
                didi.dione@dionesystems.com

Daniel G. Farley
Strategic Product Manager
Tyco Safety Products, Simplex Grinnell
50 Technology Dr.
Westminster, MA 01473
Phone: (978) 731-8497
Fax: (978) 731-8881
E-mail: dfarley@tycoint.com
Web Page: www.tycosafetyproducts-
us.com

David Holmberg
NIST
100 Bureau Drive, Stop 8631
Gaithersburg, MD 20899-8631
Phone: (301) 975-6450
E-mail: david.holmberg@nist.gov
Web Page: www.bfrl.nist.gov

Bill Ferretti
Deputy Director
Montgomery County, Maryland
9-1-1 Communications Center
Department of Police
2350 Research Boulevard
Rockville, MD 20850
Phone: (240) 773-7026
Mobile: (240) 876-1959
Fax: (240) 773-7030
E-mail:
bill.ferretti@montgomerycountymd.gov

Mike Galler
National Institute of Standards and
Technology
100 Bureau Dr
Gaithersburg, MD 20899-8631
Phone: (301) 975-6521
E-mail: michael.galler@nist.gov
Web Page: www.bfrl.nist.gov

Bill Hobgood
Project Manager, Public Safety Team
City of Richmond
Department of Information Technology
900 East Broad Street, Room 6-2
Richmond, VA 23219
Phone: (804) 646-5140
Fax: (804) 646-7048
E-mail:
        bhobgood@ci.richmond.va.us
Web Page: www.richmondgov.com

Bill Kalin
Clarus Technology
Office for Interoperability and
Compatibility
Science and Technology Directorate
Department of Homeland Security
Phone: 202-254-6774
Mobile: 703-283-2835

Keith Johnson
Battalion Chief, Assistant Fire Marshal
Fairfax County
10700 Page Avenue
Fairfax, Virginia 22030
Phone: (703) 246-4753
Fax: (703) 691-0209
E-mail:
        keith.johnson@fairfaxcounty.gov
Web Page:
www.fairfaxcounty.gov/fr/prevention

Walt Magnussen Ph.D.
Director, University
Telecommunications
Texas A&M University
College Station, TX 77843-1371
Phone: (979) 845-5588
Fax: (979) 847-1111
E-mail: telecom@tamu.edu

Scott Parker
Project Manager
IJIS Institute
44983 Knoll Square
Ashburn, VA 20147
Phone: (602) 710-1045
Mobile: (602) 616-1433
Fax: (703) 726-3557
E-mail: scott.parker@ijis.org
Web Page: www.ijis.org

Pamela J. Petrow
Chief Operating Officer
Vector Security
3400 McKnight East Dr.
Pittsburgh, PA 15237
Phone: (412) 364-2600
Fax: (412) 364-7187
E-mail:
        pjpetrow@vectorsecurity.com
Web Page: www.vectorsecurity.com

Michelle Raymond
Principal Research Scientist
Honeywell
1985 Douglas Drive North
Dock 1, MN10-112A
Golden Valley, MN 55422
Phone: (763) 954-6524
Fax: (763) 954-5489
E-mail:
        michelle.raymond@honeywell.co
m

Brian Rosen
Senior Director
Neustar
470 Conrad Drive
Mars, PA 16046
Phone: (724) 272-9172
Mobile: (724) 382-1051
E-mail: brian.rosen@neustar.biz
Web Page: www.neustar.biz

Brooke Smith
CMC National Database Mgr.
ADT
Phone: 919-570-8182
Mobile: 954-415-2495
E-mail: brookesmith@adt.com

Alan B. Vinh
NIST
100 Bureau Drive
Gaithersburg, MD 20899-8630
Phone: (301) 975-5260
Fax: (301) 975-5433
E-mail: alan.vinh@nist.gov
Web Page: www.bfrl.nist.gov

Stephen Wisely
Technical Services Manager
APCO International
351 N. Williamson Blvd.
Daytona Beach, FL 32114-1112
Phone: (386) 235-3592
Fax: (386) 322-2501
E-mail: wiselys@apcointl.org
Web Page: www.apcointl.org

Table 1: Workshop Participants

The workshop was opened with remarks from Jason Averill who welcomed the participants to NIST, reviewed the primary objectives of the meeting, walked through the basic agenda (see appendix), and allowed attendees to conduct brief self-introductions.

David Holmberg summarized the history of the relevant work that NIST has conducted prior to the workshop. Figure 1 summarizes the key topic areas and the responsible stakeholders involved in delivering building information to first responders. These areas can be categorized as involving service partners and government, groups involved with building construction,

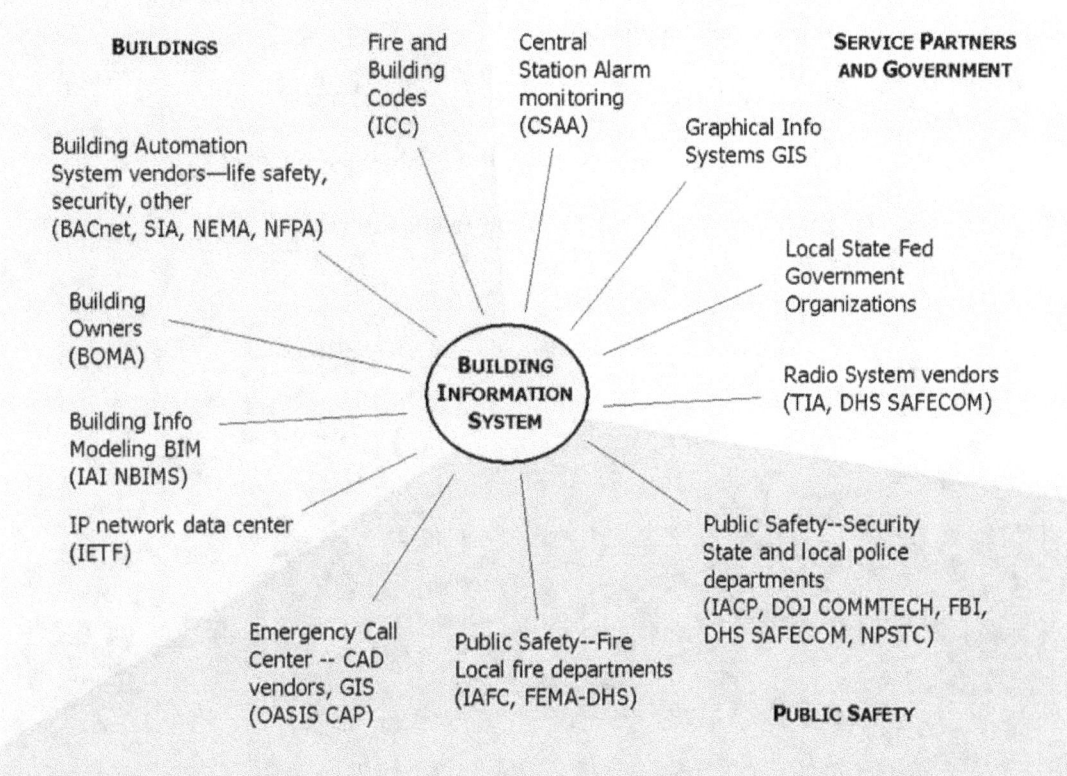

Figure 1: Stakeholders in the Building Information Exchange Process

management, and maintenance, and the public safety sector. In 2005[1] and 2006,[2] NIST hosted workshops to identify building information needs of fire and police responders, and to find "what is working" for high-rise and complex incident response communications. NIST also developed a user interface for presentation of building information to fire and police with demonstrations at NIST and in Wilson, NC, in collaboration with the Wilson Fire Department.

Holmberg also presented a high-level overview of the information flow from building sensors to emergency responder, including each interface where information requires a positive action in order to process or transfer to the emergency responder. There are key interfaces which require standardization of protocols, content, and/or authentication, including building alarm to central station alarm, central alarm to either next generation (NG) 9-1-1 or the public safety answering point, and the public safety answering point to the emergency responders (either en-route or on-scene). Additionally, emergency responders may have two-way communication and control functionality with the building through an emergency interface (such as NEMA SB30).

Holmberg concluded with identification of several specific goals, including:

- CAP, NIEM, EDXL. What are building alert communication requirements, and do the protocols satisfy these?

- What methods are required to receive alerts and query building?

- Agree on basic message elements that need to be supported.

- Agreement on extending CAP to allow event filtering.

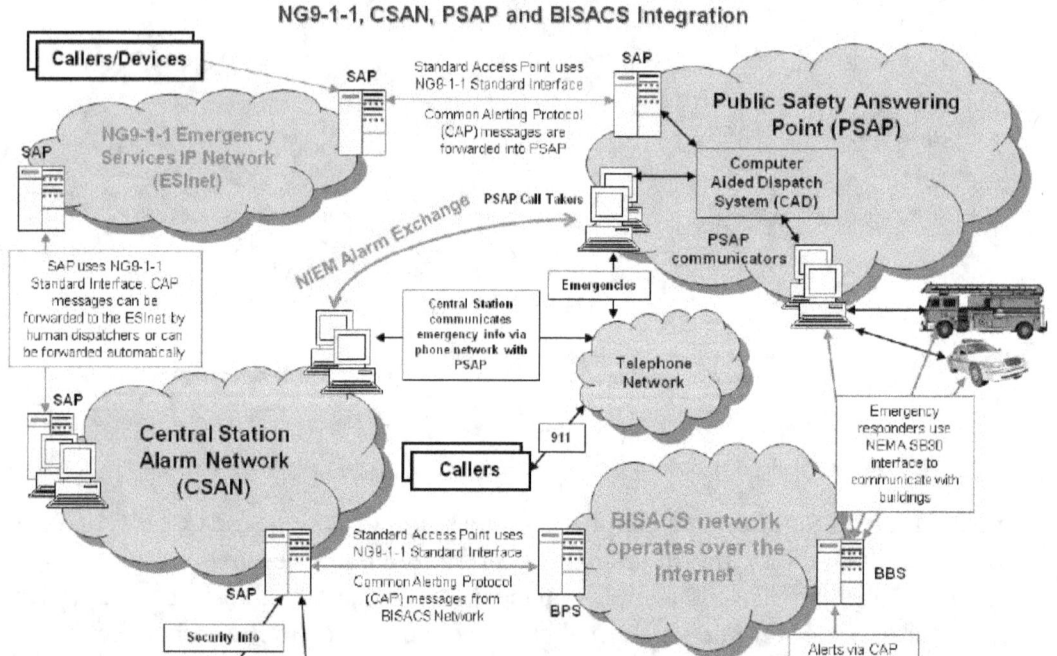

Figure 2: NIST conceptualization of the information flow from building sensors to emergency responders

- Discussion of security requirements and approaches to addressing security

- Agree on principle and outline of SAP

- How do we move forward? Identification of stakeholders and leaders to coordinate.

There was a discussion of EDXL as a wrapper which can deliver message contents in a flexible manner, which may keep options open for future enhancements to the data stream coming out of buildings. A suggestion was made that trying to pack specific information into a CAP message is not useful; rather a CAP message should simply be considered an indication that there is something wrong inside the building. A better consideration may be to establish a URI which provides detailed information about the building and the conditions within the building.

An issue for loading pre-plans for emergency management use is ensuring that the plans are (a) accurate and (b) up-to-date. The tragedy in Columbine, CO demonstrated that reliance on pre-plans which are not up-to-date can present problems in incident management. Additionally, keeping the pre-plans up-to-date can consume significant fire department resources. However, if a firefighter is going into a building for the first time and without pre-plans, they are "behind the eight ball."

Architecture

Alan Vinh led the next discussion of the flow of information. Specific discussion was focused around the NIST vision for a BISACS architecture which integrates building information. Figure 3 shows a graphical representation of the BISACS architecture.

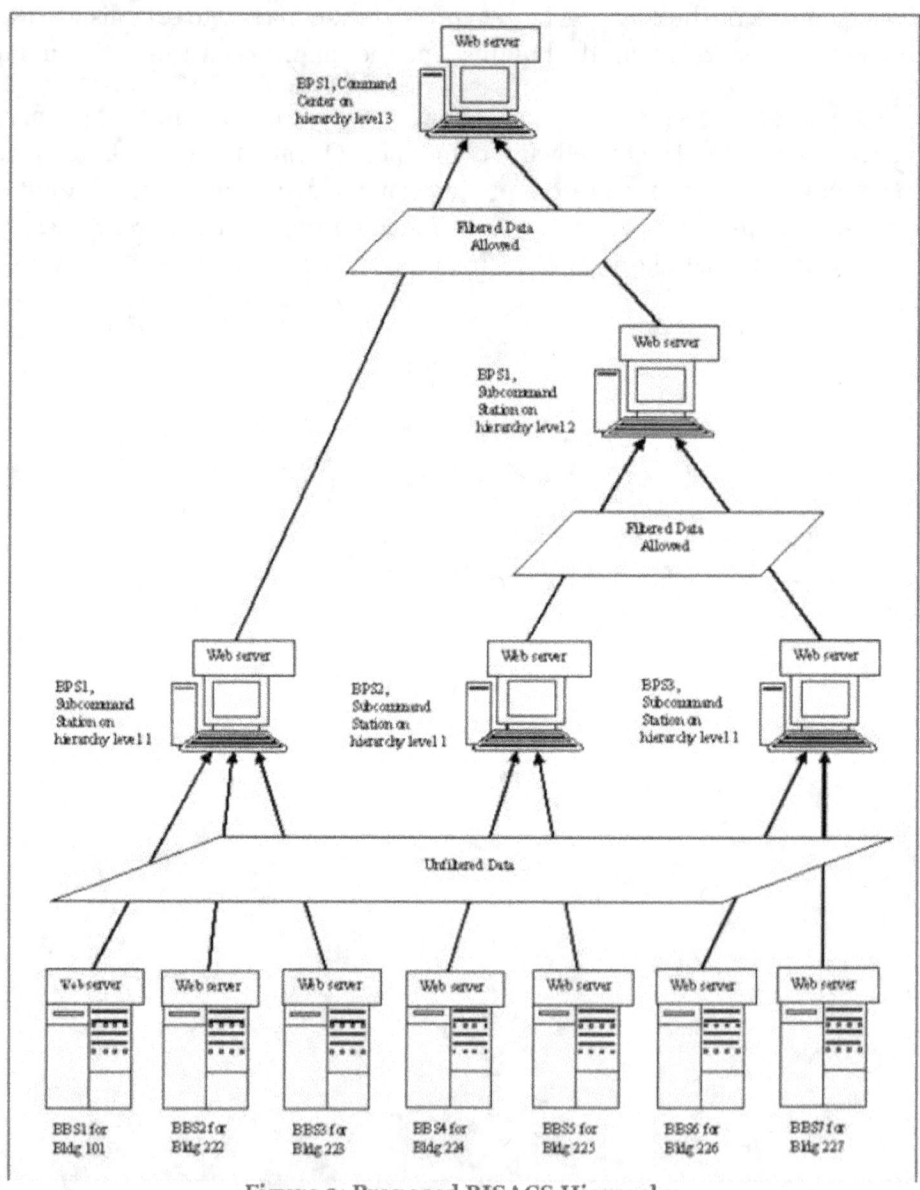

Figure 3: Proposed BISACS Hierarchy

The primary issues raised during the discussion of the BISACS architecture centered around the Building Base Server (BBS). First, it remains unclear which parties would be responsible for purchasing, installing, and maintaining the BBS. Potential parties responsible for the base servers include building owners, central standard alarm companies, or an emergent industry. Additionally, BBS-style servers are being developed for systems beyond safety and security, including energy management, smart-grid, and others. These servers are also being installed by sub-tenants within large buildings. The coordination of the servers will become increasingly important, particularly for first responders who need to disconnect utilities during emergencies.

Additional discussion included security tokens between tenants/building owners to the emergency responders in order to authorize temporary use of the camera systems for monitoring the conditions or activities inside a building. Generation of a set of business rules that determine which parties are provided access to specific sets of actions and information will be important going forward.

Vinh opened a discussion on the content and delivery of automated messages from the building to an alarm company and/or public service access point (PSAP). The initial proposed format was Common Alerting Protocol (CAP). A method for filtering the messages at the PSAP by event labels was discussed, though participants with knowledge of dispatch procedures reinforced the need for people to remain involved in the decision-making and filtering process.

Floor Plans

The issue of how to communicate floor plan information was discussed at length. The ability to spatially identify specific sensor output is critical to proper situation awareness. Transferring data over limited bandwidths may not be practical, which suggests a need to store building geometry information remotely (on fire trucks and at the dispatch centers, for example).

Access, Authentication, and Authorization

A key technical hurdle to implementing data exchange is the ability of stakeholders (including building owners and public service dispatch) to authorize and authenticate the identity of hardware and users of the systems. Creation of certificates and session keys for access to systems was discussed, though it was noted that other communities were also dealing with these issues of electronic access. Liability of allowing access (even for first responders) is a concern to the building owners.

Scenarios for compliance and design

There was discussion about whether (fire) scenarios were established in order to establish a baseline of system performance for both design and compliance testing of installed systems. While some isolated efforts have occurred, including scenarios for stadiums and mass transit, there do not appear to be standardized fire or other emergency scenarios for typical buildings.

Next-generation 9-1-1 system

Rosen presented an overview of the next-generation 9-1-1 system (NG 9-1-1) with a focus on how the pending changes might impact the flow of building information to the various stakeholders. Work is underway to transform the current telephone network-based emergency 9-1-1 system to an IP network-based emergency system (see Figure 4). NENA, APCO, and the FCC are principal amongst many organizations actively working to transition the system. There are many issues unresolved regarding who is responsible for certain activities, who is paying for the services and hardware, and when the transition will occur. However, the transition is inevitable. Trials and proof-of-concept are currently deployed and limited system availability will occur by the end of 2009. The system will essentially consist of a network-of-networks, nominally called ESI Nets or Public Safety Networks. Currently, the definition of public safety remains unresolved: e.g., school bus drivers transport many people very quickly and may or may not be considered public safety officials. There is a general unease amongst the public service access point stakeholders with respect to the number of parties that are 'tied in' to the system.

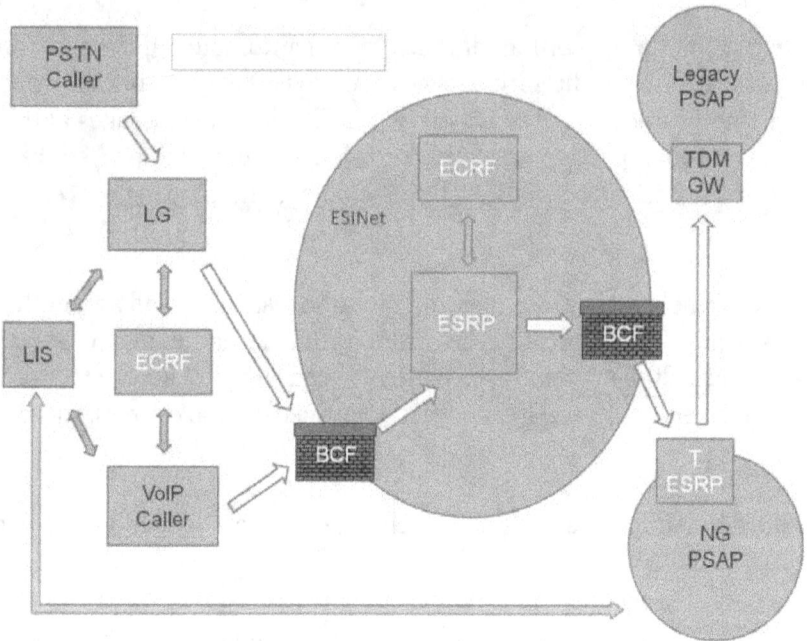

Figure 4: NG9-1-1 Network Design

NG 9-1-1 has several modules defined, including local information servers (LIS) which can return the location of a specific device. Presence Information Data Format (PIDF) can define a local address or latitude/longitude, down to the specificity of a chair in an auditorium. Emergency Call Routing Function (ECRF) is driven by GIS and can locate and dispatch responders, including the use of polygons to dynamically change routing as necessary. Border control functions serve as firewalls for the network. Emergency Services Routing Protocols are business rules that each jurisdiction can establish in order to individually manage the deployment of local responders. Third-party calls (such as OnStar, ADT, hearing impaired communication device (TTY)) are currently accepted in the proposed architecture.

Security for NG 9-1-1 is summarized by a 'trust but verify' philosophy. There will be federated PKI's for agencies; one for police and one for fire. Authorization for system interaction will be role-based. A common policy for storing and editing will be established.

Magnussen presented an overview of the NG 9-1-1 trial sites. The system is TDM-based and has PSAP sites in Washington, Montana, Minnesota, Indiana, and New York, with laboratory sites at Texas A&M University, Columbia University, and a private contractor (Booze Allen Hamilton). The backbone of Internet2 emulates an EMI network (shown in Figure 5). Richmond, VA is currently testing NG 9-1-1 with over 3,000 customers. The system processed over 64,000 signals through 300 PSAP contacts.

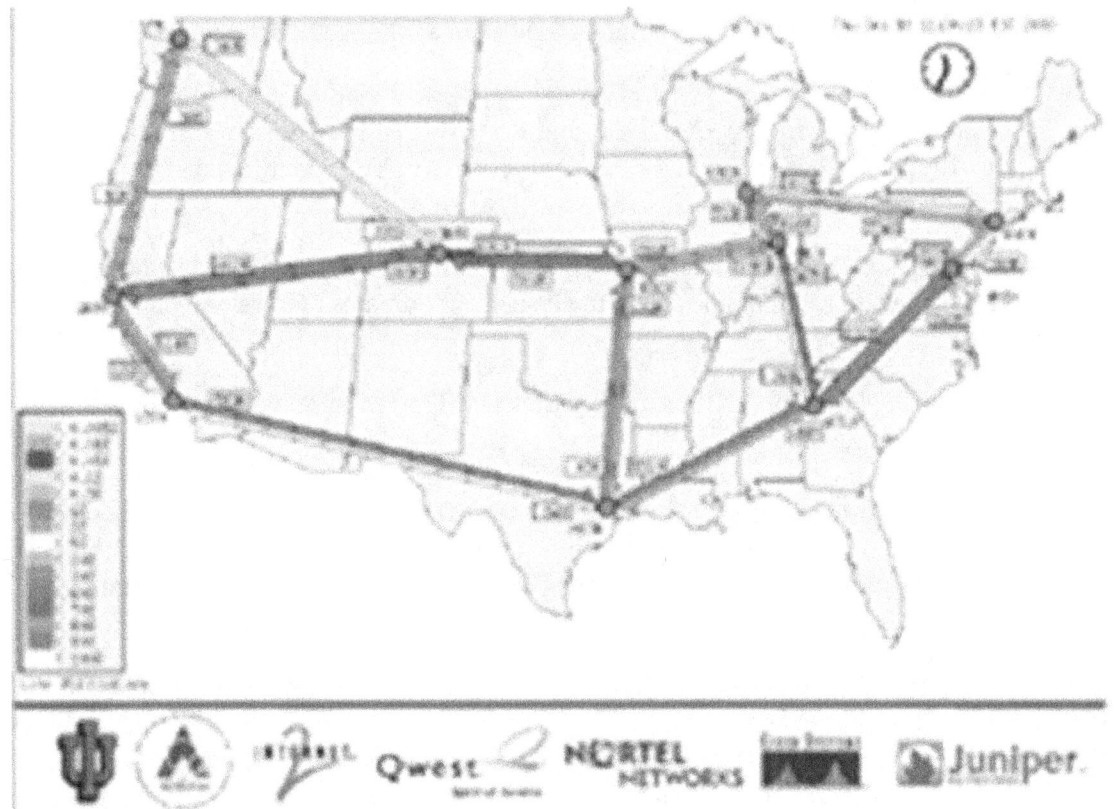

Figure 5: Internet2 Backbone Centers

Project 36 is developing a CAD to CAD interface, including an alarm data exchange which will standardize CSA to PSAP communications. The Global Justice model, in collaboration with IJIS, is now going to NIEM 2.0. The International Justice and Public Safety Network (NLETS) links state, local, federal, and international law enforcement, justice and public safety agencies to exchange critical data and may be an existing mechanism (secure VPN) to enable access to the state public safety systems.

There was a question about whether the isolated NG9-1-1 network could be switched over to a commodity network. This could only be realized with 2-3 physically diverse carriers, trenches switches, etc, in order to ensure redundancy and availability of the network.

The LoST database defines PSAP boundaries and polygons. APCO has 15,000 members at the PSAP level. CSAA is concerned with manufacturing and monitoring systems (including maintenance of UL certifications on systems). NBFAA installs and services systems.

Data Exchange Formats

Ferretti and Raymond reviewed four national models for data exchange formations: GJXDM – Global Justice XML Data Model, NIEM – National Information Exchange Model, CAP – Common Alerting Protocol, and EDXL – Emergency Data eXchange Language. XML based data reference model

Global IS Initiative is sponsored by DOJ, OJP, and BJA. GJXDM provides a common language, vocabulary, methodology, specific to justice and public safety. The widely used standard is independent of technology.

NIEM is built upon GJXDM and is sponsored by DOJ, DHS, and ODNI. NIEM is designed to extend the reach of Justice and public safety to all relevant domains, and release 2.0 is now available.

The Common Alerting Protocol (CAP) is managed by OASIS/ EMTC and sponsored by DHS/FEMA. Partners include Emergency Interoperability Consortium. CAP is a format for exchanging all-hazard emergency alerts and public warnings independent of technology and networks and is a stand-alone protocol and payload for EDXL messages. Originally designed for authority-to-public communications, CAP may be missing some elements of CAD which would inhibit ease of use by the PSAP community. However, the National Incident Management System (NIMS) has specified use of CAP or EDXL in order to be considered interoperable.

Emergency Data eXchange Language (EDXL) is managed by OASIS EMTC and is sponsored by DHS/FEMA. An XML based application, EDXL is an integrated framework designed for broad emergency data exchange applications which provides a standard message distribution framework that can be utilized over all data transport technologies (SOAP HTTP) and facilitates routing of XML formatted emergency messages. The value of the EDXL wrapper for emergency messages are that it establishes connectivity, can be archived, associated, tracked, and then subsequently used in after-action reports. Identifiers are required in order to link the data, along with standardized logging protocols. An overarching goal of many of these formats is to make the messages so 'lightweight' that it will encourage users to 'log everything.'

Parker presented an overview of the National Information Exchange Model (NIEM). There are 124 Tier 1 (e.g., New York City) and Tier 2 (e.g., Richmond) CAD providers and thousands of developers. Nationally, there are 6,500 PSAPs, with 85 percent having five or fewer positions. The majority are governed by law enforcement agencies. NIEM consists of (a) data dictionary of agreed-to terms and definitions; object oriented data model providing components for creating Information Exchange Packages (IEP); set of specifications for building NIEM components and IEPs; governance processes and support infrastructure; clearinghouse of reusable IEP documentation (IEPD); online web-based tools for building IEPDs; and represents a partnership of local, state, tribal, and federal entities. Hobgood presented an overview of the NIEM structures (see Figure 6). Currently, NIEM consists of seven domains – emergency management, infrastructure protection, immigration, intelligence, person screening, justice, and international trade. At the core of the standard are people, places, things (e.g., property, metadata), and events. DHS and DoJ sometimes require compliance with NIEM standards for certain solicitations, along with CAP and EDXL. Additional information can be found at http://www.niem.gov.

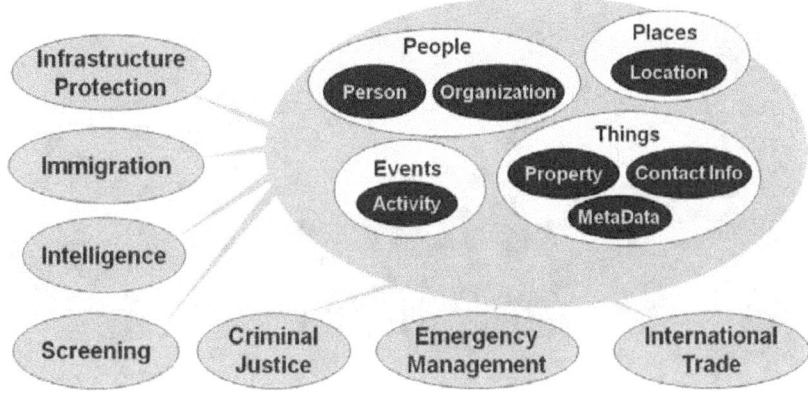

Figure 6: Overview of NIEM Structure

During the lunch break, Coggeshall conducted a DMIS demonstration using EDXL. With Google maps, the developers added information about the location of fire departments, water mains, Red Cross relief stations, and other relevant GIS-based information. The system can track (in real-time) information about the location and status of resources and can dynamically reroute the assets as appropriate.

After lunch, Raymond presented an overview of the NEMA SB30 (see Figure 7) panel, which standardizes the building interface for the first responders. Recently adopted into the NFPA 72 annex, the SB30 standard will facilitate rapid assessment of building conditions by the incident commander. Additionally, standardization of information is helpful to industry because it allows the industry to focus on adding value to the products rather than worrying about the format of the data. SB30 version 2.0 will create display equipment standards for design, operation, arrangement of information, certain control functions, and address portable displays. Presently, NEMA SB30 Building Interface Task Group is developing standards for remotely controlling building functions, including communication connectivity, security (authentication and credentialing), and information format. Significant remaining issues also include (a) determining who has access to what information, when they are authorized for access, and where the access points will be located, and (b) developing security measures for data during transmission and storage.

Figure 7: NEMA SB30 Firefighter Panel

Control

Control of building systems is the logical extension of passively reporting building sensor system data. However, in order to enable user-control of building functions, several issues must be resolved regarding the rights of the user to access and control the functions. First, the systems must recognize that an event is occurring (through automatic sensors systems or through manual activation). Based upon the event, role-based authorization for users must be defined. ESRP or LoST can control the level of access of different users based on their role in the event. The roles can be managed through federated identity management (establishment of the user's identity across IT systems). For fire/police service access this would likely be managed at the department level rather than at the building level. It was noted that building owners have significant concerns about allowing access to building systems and strong policies and security will be necessary to overcome these objections. Creating logs of network activities (who, what and when information was accessed and or transferred) will also ensure accountability and traceability during and after an event. NG 9-1-1 has developed simple web-based logging protocols which are distributed but can readily be reassembled for post-event review.

There was a discussion of the appropriateness of personnel located off-site being authorized to initiate building control functions. There was a general consensus that on-site personnel have better situation awareness and should be the preferred control agents; however, certain scenarios may preclude effective operations by on-site personnel (such as a toxic cloud around a building). Therefore, off-site control functionality should be strongly considered.

Additionally, if authorization for an individual to have access to the building information and control functions is event-based, there was a discussion about how the authorization would be revoked. If the authorization were time-based, how would events which require additional time be 'renewed?' As a converse to the revocation issue, an event should be able to be manually created; in other words, authorization and access should be allowed even if the building does not 'know' that there is an event inside.

There was a discussion about the need for identifiers. Identifiers include agencies, agents, and incidents. Incidents must be hierarchical with merge and split capabilities as there may be multiple streams and sources of data for an incident. With respect to sources of data, three types of communications were identified: citizen to authority alerts (such as a 9-1-1 call reporting an event); authority to authority alerts (such as a warning of a possible future event); and authority to citizen alerts (such as a broadcast to citizens that there is a tornado on the ground).

Hobgood reviewed the experience of Richmond, VA as a testbed for usage of NIEMS data. Richmond eliminated over 5,000 emergency calls; extrapolated nationwide this could translate to a reduction of over 32 million emergency calls. The issue of responsibility for conforming the many agencies relative to data exchange was discussed. The Federal government has led by tying grant money to NIEMS compliance, which forces local responders to comply with the standards. A resource for local governments, including toolkits, can be found at http://www.safecomprogram.gov/SAFECOM/. However, these requirements have changed several times (for example, CAP became GJXML which became NIEM) and private sector has borne the cost of reprogramming for each change.

The value and use of data requirements was discussed. As more data is required or available, the potential for liability or misuse increases. Therefore, each element should be carefully reviewed to ensure that the value exceeds the cost of inclusion.

Day 2

The opening discussion centers around using Uniform Markup Language to specify elements that are key to success. It would provide a framework for moving the choice of exchange language forward. Additionally, the layers of data exchange were discussed:

- Content: XML
- Inner Wrapper: CAP, EXDL
- Routing and Addressing: SIP, WSDL
- Transport: TCP, TLS

Holmberg proposes roles for each stakeholder as the project proceeds. For the CAP format, a policy which combines preset roles with scenarios in a template format is required, along with security and event type definitions. Raymond is identified to lead floorplan standardization (including possible use of OGC form of geolocation to offset from a known location). Magnussen is identified to investigate private or open network communications. Holmberg will identify building control functions. Averill will work with NEMA to move the next generation of the SB 30 panel forward. NENA is standardizing the addressing and validation requirements. Parker will work with IJIS security and privacy advisory committee to ensure that issues raised during the workshop will be considered by the working group.

Remaining Technical Issues

Several issues remain unaddressed, including:

- Ownership and maintenance of databases;
- Whether Block D availability will increase bandwidth possibilities for information exchange; review of inspection requirements of the new systems and whether automation can ease the burden on fire marshals.
- CAP fields should use existing terms to the extent possible.
- Hosting a disaster walk-through with many stakeholders starting with a single sensor activation would be beneficial format to identify and work unanticipated issues.
- Criteria to route calls based on the content of the message should be established.
- Bi-directional interfaces that use URL's to point to data are a potential alternative to sending all information in a single packet.
- Using certificates to authenticate communications may be challenged by the need to reroute calls to alternative locations.
- Building owners need to be engaged to ensure that their concerns are addressed well in advance of codes and standards development work. It is likely that owners will be accepting if the systems are secure, tested, and able to be manually turned off.
- Managing corporate firewalls will be an issue for ensuring the full flow of data.
- Security authentication should consider two-factor authentication such as a password and a biometric.
- Multihazard scenarios for system design and compliance should be developed.
- The implications of new data exchange systems regarding UL certification should be considered.

References

[1] Jones, W. W.; Holmberg, D. G.; Davis, W. D.; Bushby, S. T.; Reed, K. A. Workshop to Define Information Needed by Emergency Responders During Building Emergencies. National Institute of Standards and Technology, Gaithersburg, MD. NISTIR 7193; 34 p. January 2005.

[2] Vettori, R. L.; Lawson, J. R.; Davis, W. D.; Holmberg, D. G.; Bushby, S. T. "High-Rise and Large/Complex Incident Communications Workshop. National Institute of Standards and Technology, Gaithersburg, MD. NIST Technical Note 1479; 104 p. February 2007.

Appendix A. List of Acronyms

ADSL – Asymmetrical Digital Subscriber Line

AIA – American Institute of Architects

ALI – Automatic Location Identification (a.k.a. ALI/ANI or ANI/ALI)

ANI – Automatic Number Identification (a.k.a. ALI/ANI or ANI/ALI)

ANSI – American National Standards Institute

APCO – Association of Public Safety Communications Officials

ASCII – American Standard Code for Information Interchange

ATM – Asynchronous Transfer Mode

AVL – Automatic Vehicle Location

BACnet – Building Automation and Control Network

BBS – BISACS Base Server

BJA – Bureau of Justice Assistance

BPS – BISACS Proxy Server

BIM – Building Information Model/Modeling

BIS – Building Information System

BISACS – Building Information Services and Control System

BOMA – Building Owners and Managers Association

CAD – Computer Aided Dispatch

CAP – Common Alerting Protocol

CIQ – Customer Information Quality

CLLI – Common Language Location Identifier

CityGML – City Geography Markup Language

CSAA – Central Station Alarm Association (a.k.a. CSA for short)

CSAN – Central Station Alarm Network

DBMS – Data Base Management System

DCE – Data Communications Equipment

DHCP – Dynamic Host Control Protocol, Dynamic Host Configuration Protocol

DoS – Denial of Service

DHS – US Department of Homeland Security

DMIS – Disaster Management Interoperability Services

DNS – Domain Name Server

DOE – US Department of Energy

DOJ – US Department of Justice

DOJ COMMTECH – US Department of Justice, Communications Technology

DOT – US Department of Transportation

DSL – Digital Subscriber Line

DTE – Data Terminal Equipment

E9-1-1 – Enhanced 9-1-1

EAS – Emergency Alert System

ebXML Registry-Repository – Electronic Business using eXtensible Markup Language

ECC – Emergency Communications Center (associated with PSAP)

EDXL – Emergency Data Exchange Language

EDXL-DE – Emergency Data Exchange Language Distribution Element

EDXL-RM – Emergency Data Exchange Language Resource Messaging

EDXL-HAVE – Emergency Data Exchange Language Hospital Availability Exchange

EIA – Electronic Industry Association

EMS – Emergency Medical Service

ESINet – Emergency Services IP Network

FBI – Federal Bureau of Investigation

FCC – Federal Communications Commission

FEMA – Federal Emergency Management Agency

FTP – File Transfer Protocol

FR – First Responder

GEO-OASIS – Profile of GML for use with OASIS Specifications

GeoX3D – GeoPositionInterpolator Node of X3D

GIS – Geographic Information System

GJXDM – Global Justice XML Data Model

GML – Geography Markup Language

GMT – Greenwich Mean Time (a.k.a. UTC time or Zulu time)

GPS – Global Positioning System

HTTP – Hypertext Transfer Protocol

HTTPS – Secured Hypertext Transfer Protocol

HVAC – Heating, Ventilation and Air Conditioning

IACP – International Association of Chiefs of Police

IAFC – International Association of Fire Chiefs

IAI – International Alliance for Interoperability

IANA – Internet Assigned Numbers Authority

IC – Incident Commander

ICC – International Code Council

IEEE – Institute of Electrical and Electronic Engineers

IEPD – Information Exchange Package Document

IESG – Internet Engineering Steering Group

IETF – Internet Engineering Task Force

IFC – Industry Foundation Classes

IJIS – Integrated Justice Information Sharing Institute (a.k.a. IJIS Institute)

IP – Internet Protocol

ISDN – Integrated Services Digital Network

ISP – Internet Service Provider

ITSP – Internet Telephone Service Provider

JPEG – Joint Photographic Experts Group

LAN – Local Area Network
LEC – Local Exchange Carrier
LED – Light Emitting Diode
LCD – Liquid Crystal Display
LoST – Location to Service Translation
MDC – Mobile Data Computer (a.k.a. Mobile Data/Digital Communicator)
NAI – Network Access Identifier
NAS – Network Access Server
NAT – Network Access Translation
NBIMS – National Building Information Model/Modeling Standard
NCIC – National Crime Information Center, National Crime Enforcement Center
NEMA – National Electrical Manufacturers Association
NENA – National Emergency Number Association
NFPA – National Fire Protection Association
NG9-1-1 – Next Generation 9-1-1 (a.k.a. NG for short)
NIBS – National Institute of Building Science
NIEM – National Information Exchange Model
NIST – National Institute of Standards and Technology
NPSTC – National Public Safety Telecommunications
NRTL – Nationally Recognized Testing Laboratory
NTP – Network Time Protocol
OASIS – Organization for the Advancement of Structured Information Standards
oBIX – Open Building Information Xchange
PIV Card – Personal Identity Verification Card
PKI – Public Key Infrastructure
PPP – Point-to-Point Protocol
PPPoA – Point-to-Point over Asynchronous Transfer Protocol (ATM)
PPPoE – Point-to-Point over Ethernet
PSAP – Public Safety Answering Point (associated with ECC)
PSTN – Public Switched Telephone Network
QoS – Quality of Service
RAID – Redundant Array of Independent Disks
RTCP – Real Time Control Protocol
RTP – Real Time Transport Protocol
RTSP – Real Time Streaming Protocol
SAFECOM – Communications Program of DHS's Office for Interoperability and Compatibility
SAP – Standard Access Point
SDO – Standards Development Organization
SDSL – Symmetrical Digital Subscriber Line
SensorML – Sensor Markup Language
SI – Services Interface (in the context of BISACS)
SIA – Security Industry Association

SHA – Secure Hash Algorithm
SIP – Session Initiation Protocol
SMS – Short Message Service
SOA – Service Oriented Architecture
SOA-RM – Reference Model for Service Oriented Architecture

Appendix B. Workshop Agenda

October 15, 2008

9:00 a.m.   Overview and Welcome (Averill)

9:15 a.m.   NIST's Overall Vision of Building Information Flow (Holmberg)

9:45 a.m.   Stakeholder Presentations

- BISACS Overview
- Central Station Overview
- Next Generation 9-1-1 Overview
- APCO Project 36 Overview
- Emergency Command Center Overview
- SB30 Overview

Noon   Lunch

1:00 p.m.   Panel Discussion on Technical Issues

- PSAP Network Interface
- Communication Protocols

5:00 p.m.   Adjourn

October 16, 2008

9:00 a.m.   Panel Discussion on Technical Issues

- Data Encapsulation
- Security

Noon   Lunch

1:00 p.m.   Further Discussion, Summary and Next Steps

3:00 p.m.   Adjourn

Appendix C. Presentations

Building Information Services and Control System (BISACS), a Framework For a Safer Tomorrow

Alan Vinh

Building Environment Division
Building and Fire Research Laboratory
National Institute of Standards and Technology
United States Department of Commerce

October 15, 2008

Introduction

How can building information help us construct a safer tomorrow?

Modern buildings can support vast amount of static and real-time data that can be used for emergency scenarios:

- Real-time sensors such as temperature, smoke, motion, lighting, doors, elevators, various HVAC controllers and electrical information, and video cameras, are readily available
- Static information such as building floor plans and hazardous material information can be made available

1) Make building alerts and building information available
2) Route this information to the proper authorities
3) Give those authorities the ability to look back into our buildings

We can do a better job of saving lives and properties in emergency situations

---

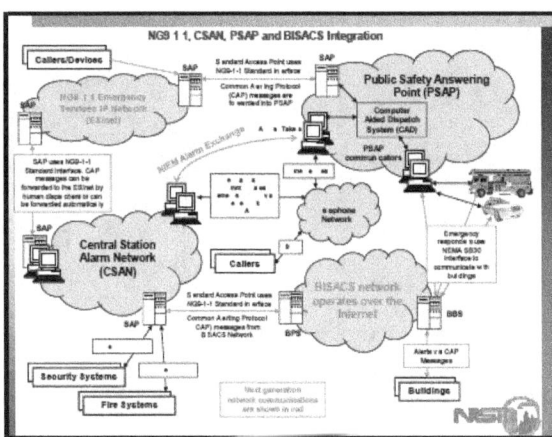

NG9 1 1, CSAN, PSAP and BISACS Integration

Alerts and Alarms

- Alerts are signals from sensor devices. When alerts convey abnormal conditions, then they become alarms.

- Alert signals are transformed into human readable XML messages via the Common Alerting Protocol (CAP).

- The Building Information Services and Control System (BISACS) propagates the CAP messages via its network of servers.

Building Information Services And Control System (BISACS)

- The BISACS is a network of computers and software – made up of Base Servers and Proxy Servers

- Alerts or alarms are sent from these computers up the network hierarchy

- The communication is encrypted and secured

- User authentication and authorization is required to communicate with these servers

- Future plans include the ability to send commands to buildings such as commands to shut off utilities.

BISACS, Up Close

- The BISACS Base Server (BBS) controls one or more networks of devices

- Alerts or alarms are generated by the Services Interfaces (SI) and sent to the BBS via CAP messages

- Alerts and alarms are collected at the BISACS Proxy Servers (BPS)

- The BPS can be monitored by the PSAP or they can inject these alerts into the Standard Access Point of another public safety network

- First responders can log back into the BBS and look at various building information to better assess the emergency scenarios. Future plans include the ability to send commands to buildings such as commands to shut off utilities.

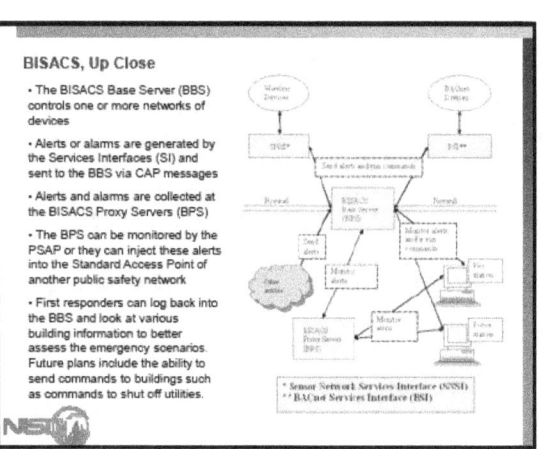

* Sensor Network Services Interface (SNSI)
** BACnet Services Interface (BSI)

Sample Common Alerting Protocol Message from a Building

```xml
<?xml version "1.0" encoding "UTF-8"?>
<alert xmlns "urn oasis names tc emergency cap 1.1">
  <identifier>1179353147004 2</identifier>
  <sender>https //cybute1.nist.gov 8443/bisacs</sender>
  <sent>2008-09-16T18 05 47-04 00</sent>
  <status>Exercise</status>
  <msgType>Alert</msgType>
  <source>alarm1bundle.sensor01</source>
  <scope>Public</scope>
  <info>
    <category>Env</category>
    <category>Fire</category>
    <category>Health</category>
    <category>Rescue</category>
    <category>Safety</category>
    <category>Security</category>
    <event>Smoke</event>
    <urgency>Immediate</urgency>
    <severity>Extreme</severity>
    <certainty>Observed</certainty>
    <expires>2008-09-16T18 06 47-04 00</expires>
    <description>Smoke detector, building 226, 3rd floor, room B346.</description>
  </info>
</alert>
```

Routing the Alerts

- The Central Station Alarm Association (CSAA), previews the alerts and determines their validity and priority
- The National Emergency Number Association (NENA), functions as the routing service to reach the proper Public Safety Answering Point (PSAP)
- Building alerts that have escalated to alarms are first sent to the Central Station Alarm Network so that the CSAA officials can verify and prioritize the information
- Once verified and prioritized, the alarms are forwarded to the NG9-1-1 Network for routing to the appropriate PSAP

Logging Back Into the Building

- Alarms are forwarded from the NG9-1-1 system to the PSAP
- These alarms contain Uniform Resource Locator (URL) information for the PSAP dispatch officials to log back into the originating BISACS Base Server (BBS) for further analysis of the emergency scenarios
- First responders such as fire fighters, medics and the police are dispatched to the scene appropriately
- First responders that are destined for the scene can also log into the originating BBS to plan their course of action
- The building information can show exactly where the emergency is and what precaution must be used to save lives and properies

Conclusion

1) By making building alerts and building information available
2) By routing this information to the proper authorities
3) By giving those authorities the ability to look back into our buildings

We CAN help the first responder community do a better job of saving lives and properties in emergency situations.

BFRL is working with industry to realize a safer tomorrow for us all.

Slide 1

Protocols and Message Contents - Discussion

Alan Vinh

Building Environment Division
Building and Fire Research Laboratory
National Institute of Standards and Technology
United States Department of Commerce

October 15, 2008

Slide 2

Sample Common Alerting Protocol Message from a Building

```
<?xml version "1.0" encoding "UTF-8"?>
<alert xmlns "urn oasis names tc emergency cap 1.1">
 <identifier>1179353147004 2</identifier>
 <sender>https //cybute1.nist.gov 8443/bisacs</sender>
 <sent>2008-09-16T18 05 47-04 00</sent>
 <status>Exercise</status>
 <msgType>Alert</msgType>
 <source>alarm1bundle.sensor01</source>
 <scope>Public</scope>
 <info>
  <category>Env</category>
  <category>Fire</category>
  <category>Health</category>
  <category>Rescue</category>
  <category>Safety</category>
  <category>Security</category>
  <event>Smoke</event>
  <urgency>Immediate</urgency>
  <severity>Extreme</severity>
  <certainty>Observed</certainty>
  <expires>2008-09-16T18 06 47-04 00</expires>
  <description>Smoke detector, building 226, 3rd floor, room B346. </description>
 </info>
</alert>
```

Slide 3

Common Alerting Protocol Message from a Building (continue)

What we currently have:

- Unique Message Identifier
- Time stamp of message and its expiration
- Sender/server URL for call back purposes
- Source, the unique identifier of the sensor/device that initiated the alert/alarm
- Category(ies) for filtering purposes
- Event type for filtering purposes
- Status/message type/scope/urgency/severity/certainty, i.e. all "required" fields from CAP
- Description of the event

What else is needed? We need to keep the alert message light weight.

- Location of the sensor/device -> standardized mechanism is needed, geo-location?
- Address of building -> standardized fields (e.g., address1, address2, city, state, country, zip, etc.)
- What else is needed?

Slide 4

Sample Service Request Destined for a Building - Discussion

Sample request for the floorplan of a building:
```
<?xml version "1.0" encoding "UTF-8"?>
<serviceRequest>
 <identifier>2279353147006 4</identifier>
 <fromSender>https //cybute1.nist.gov 8443/bisacs</fromSender>
 <sent>2008-10-02T15 05 47-04 00</sent>
 <requestType>getValue</requestType>
 <target>floorplan.F2</target>
</serviceRequest>
```

Sample response from the building:
```
<?xml version "1.0" encoding "UTF-8"?>
<serviceResponse>
 <identifier>2279353147006 4</identifier>
 <toSender>https //cybute1.nist.gov 8443/bisacs</toSender>
 <sent>2008-10-02T15 05 50-04 00</sent>
 <requestType>getValue</requestType>
 <source>floorplan.F2</source>
 <parameter>
  <valueName> </valueName>
  <value> The XML representation of floor 2 goes here *** </value>
 </parameter>
</serviceResponse>
```

*** How do we represent a standard floor plan so that we could run print it on the screen AND so that we can give this vendor the "standardized" location information for a sensor that can be easily mapped in this floorplan?

Slide 5

Sample Service Request Destined for a Building (continue)

Sample request for the temperature of a sensor:
```
<?xml version "1.0" encoding "UTF-8"?>
<serviceRequest>
 <identifier>2279353147006 4</identifier>
 <fromSender>https //cybute1.nist.gov 8443/bisacs</fromSender>
 <sent>2008-10-02T15 05 47-04 00</sent>
 <requestType>getValue</requestType>
 <target>alarm1bundle.sensor01</target>
 <parameter>
  <valueName>temperature.node 1</valueName>
 </parameter>
</serviceRequest>
```

Sample response from the sensor:
```
<?xml version "1.0" encoding "UTF-8"?>
<serviceResponse>
 <identifier>2279353147006 4</identifier>
 <toSender>https //cybute1.nist.gov 8443/bisacs</toSender>
 <sent>2008-10-02T15 05 50-04 00</sent>
 <requestType>getValue</requestType>
 <source>alarm1bundle.sensor01</source>
 <parameter>
  <valueName>temperature node 1</valueName>
  <value>72.4 F</value>
 </parameter>
</serviceResponse>
```

Slide 6

Sample Service Request Destined for a Building (continue)

Sample request for setting a value of a sensor:
```
<?xml version "1.0" encoding "UTF-8"?>
<serviceRequest>
 <identifier>2279353147006 4</identifier>
 <fromSender>https //cybute1.nist.gov 8443/bisacs</fromSender>
 <sent>2008-10-02T15 05 47-04 00</sent>
 <requestType>getValue</requestType>
 <target>controller1.dev02</target>
 <parameter>
  <valueName>valve gps</valueName>
  <value> </value>
 </parameter>
</serviceRequest>
```

Sample response from the sensor – it echoes the actual value that was set:
```
<?xml version "1.0" encoding "UTF-8"?>
<serviceResponse>
 <identifier>2279353147006 4</identifier>
 <toSender>https //cybute1.nist.gov 8443/bisacs</toSender>
 <sent>2008-10-02T15 05 50-04 00</sent>
 <requestType>setValue</requestType>
 <source>controller1.dev02</source>
 <parameter>
  <valueName>valve gps 1</valueName>
  <value> </value>
 </parameter>
</serviceResponse>
```

Sample Service Request Destined for a Building (continue)

Sample request for the location of hazardous materials:

```xml
<?xml version "1.0" encoding "UTF-8"?>
<serviceRequest>
  <identifier>2279353147006 4</identifier>
  <fromSender>https //cybute1.nist.gov 8443/bisacs</fromSender>
  <sent>2008-10-02T15 05 47-04 00</sent>
  <requestType>getValue</requestType>
  <target>hazmat.location</target>
</serviceRequest>
```

Sample response from the building:

```xml
<?xml version "1.0" encoding "UTF-8"?>
<serviceResponse>
  <identifier>2279353147006 4</identifier>
  <toSender>https //cybute1.nist.gov 8443/bisacs</toSender>
  <sent>2008-10-02T15 05 50-04 00</sent>
  <requestType>getValue</requestType>
  <source>hazmat.location</source>
  <parameter>
    <valueName>B1</valueName>
    <value>Room B101, Oxygen containers</value>
  </parameter>
  <parameter>
    <valueName>A2</valueName>
    <value>Room A206, Hydrochloric acid containers, gasoline containers.</value>
  </parameter>
</serviceResponse>
```

NIST

CAD Provider Perspective

Scott Parker, IJIS Institute

CAD Provider Environment

Providers
- 124+ Tier 1 & 2
- ? Custom / Desktop Developers

Customers (PSAPs)
- 6,500+
- Most Governed by LE

Development Style

- Standards *(use & reuse to keep costs low …NIEM)*
- Avoid "one-offs"
- Reuse Current Tools / Interfaces
- Use Familiar Technology

Drivers of Development

- Customer Funded *(LE grants require NIEM)*
- Competitive Need *("everyone else has it")*
- Marketing Advantage

DOJ Grant Language (DHS has similar):
"To support public safety and justice information sharing, OJP requires the grantee to use the National Information Exchange Model specifications and guidelines for this particular grant."

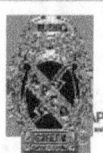 

APCO/CSAA IJIS Alert's Team
Electronic Data Transfer Project
NIST Building Information Exchange
October 15, 2008

APCO International

- World's oldest and largest professional organization dedicated to the enhancement of public safety communications
- Serves 15,000 members
- Provides leadership; influences public safety communications decisions of government and industry; promotes professional development; and, fosters the development and use of technology for the benefit of the public.
- www.apcointl.org

CENTRAL STATION ALARM ASSOCIATION

- Alarm trade association representing providers, users, bureaus, and other agencies of UL-Listed and/or FM-Approved Central Station protection services.
- Purpose
  - *"To foster and maintain the relationship among providers, users, bureaus, and other agencies of UL-Listed and/or FM-Approved Central Station protection services, and*
  - *to promote the mutual interests of the UL-Listed and/or FM-Approved Central Station alarm industry with public officials, the insurance industry and our customers."*
- www.csaaul org

Project History

- Project 36
- 6/05 APCO & CSAA entered into Alarm Data Exchange Interface Development Project Agreement
- 11/05 APCO/IJIS announced agreement to use Global Justice model
  - Effort to get away from custom interfaces for CAD systems
- 9/06 Alerts IEPD 2.0 approved
- Conversion to NIEM 2.0 to be covered later

Alerts IEPD Overview

- Supports exchange from an external source (i.e. alarm company system or other sensor) into a CAD system where a message may be for informational purposes or may be to request an emergency response. The two primary parties in the communication exchange are the dispatch requesting agency (typically a central station alarm company) and the public safety agency (typically a Communications Center (PSAP), police, fire or EMS departments) . The goals of this exchange include:
  - Reduce overall response time for alarm-based calls-for-service
  - Decrease errors in delivery of alarm and calls-for-service by eliminating voice delivery and PSAP call taker CAD re-entry
  - Reduce number of calls from central stations to PSAPS
  - Progress toward a standard for interfaces between monitoring stations and PSAPs to reduce cross-agency and cross-vendor data exchange development time and cost

---

Proof of Concept

- Participating Parties
  - York County PSAP
  - Vector Security/GE MASterMind software
  - City of Richmond Communications Center (PSAP)
  - Bill Hodgood CAD custom interface (Richmond PSAP)
- Initial Scope
  - Burglary only
  - Electronic transmission with voice back-up
- Expanded Scope
  - All alarm types (burglary, fire and medical)

Moving to the IJIS Model

- GE MasterMind needed to recode the interface to IJIS approved schema
- New CAD Installations
  - Richmond City - Intergraph
  - York County - Global Justice (Motorola)
- End of October was new test / conversion date

Communications Options

- Internet
- Third Party administered registration servers
- Intrado
- NLETS

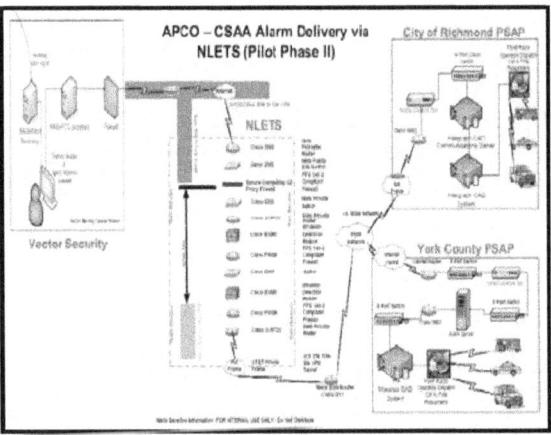

Pilot Phase II

- Virginia State Police
  - Richmond City
  - York County
- Creating VPN tunnel between NLETS and Vector
- NAT rules were requested by the PSAPS
- Testing late October 2007
- Live Fall of 2007

Thank You

Pam Petrow, Vector Security, CSAA Representative
Stephen J. Wisely, APCO International

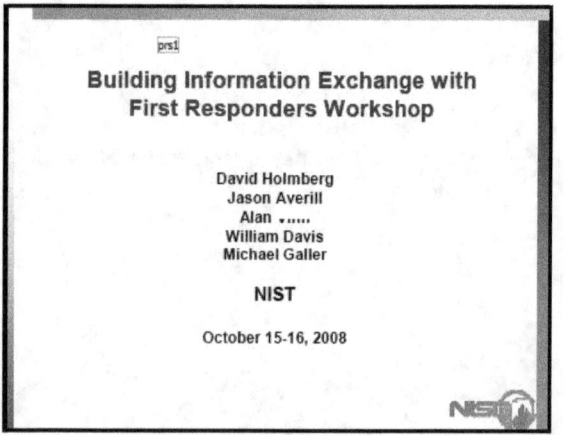

Building Information Exchange with First Responders Workshop

David Holmberg
Jason Averill
Alan ....
William Davis
Michael Galler

NIST

October 15-16, 2008

Workshop Objective

Engage key stakeholders in a dialogue on the delivery of building information to the first responder communities in order to identify opportunities for collaboration and standardization.

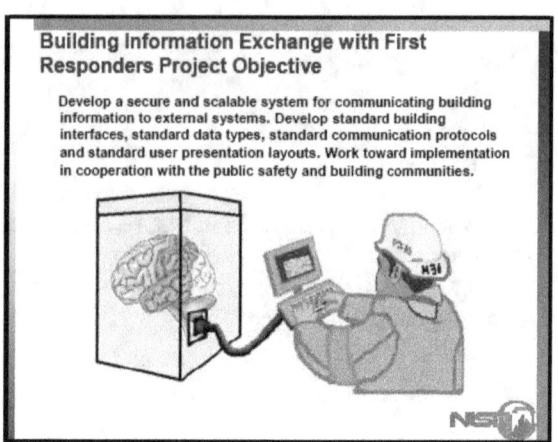

Building Information Exchange with First Responders Project Objective

Develop a secure and scalable system for communicating building information to external systems. Develop standard building interfaces, standard data types, standard communication protocols and standard user presentation layouts. Work toward implementation in cooperation with the public safety and building communities.

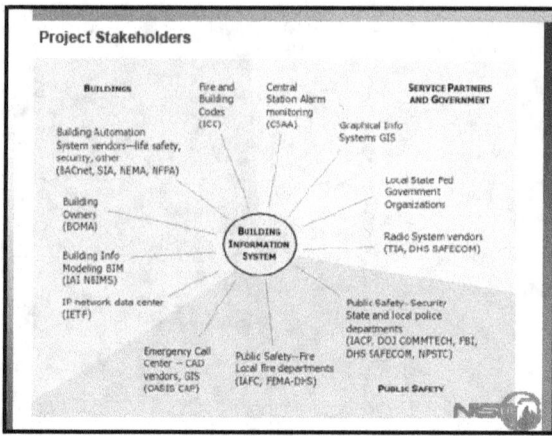

Project Stakeholders

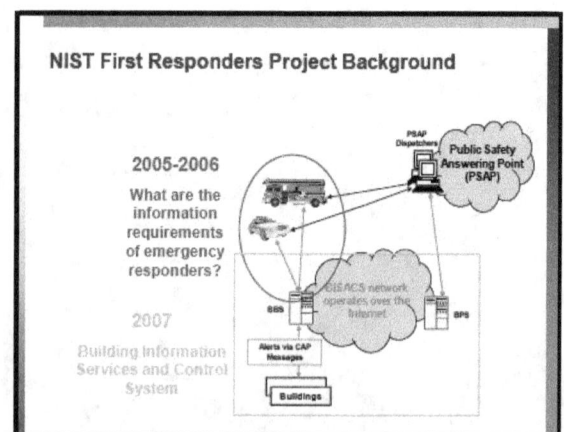

NIST First Responders Project Background

2005-2006

What are the information requirements of emergency responders?

2007

Building Information Services and Control System

Work so far

Up to this point we have made significant progress:
- Hosted workshops to identify building information needs of fire and police responders, and to find "what is working" for high-rise and complex incident response communications.
- Developed a user interface for presentation of building information to fire and police with demonstrations at NIST and in Wilson, NC.
- Produced a video with distribution count past 15,000
- NEMA SB-30 2005 standard for remote fire panel display.
- Investigated the potential for moving first responder communications over existing building networks.
- Worked with SAFECOM to address the role of buildings in the SAFECOM Statement of Requirements.
- Completed implementation of a first generation Building Information Services And Control System (BISACS) using building alerts encapsulated in the OASIS Common Alerting Protocol (CAP).

prs1   Last year each person was scheduled 15 minutes + 5 minutes for Q&A
svincek, 6/21/2007

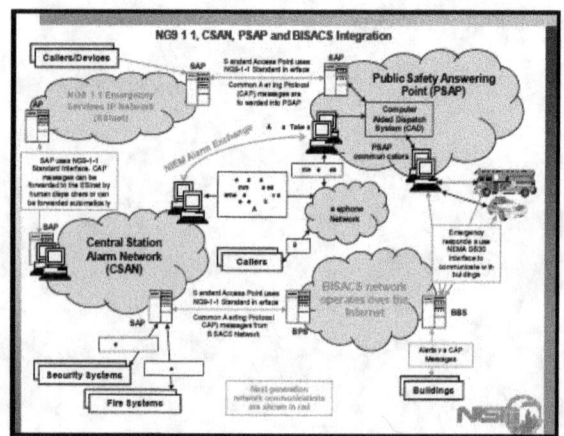

NG9 1 1, CSAN, PSAP and BISACS Integration

Workshop goals

- For this morning: hear from the different stakeholders and understand the different perspectives and efforts.
- Wed afternoon: protocols and message contents
  - CAP, NIEM, EDXL. What are building alert communication requirements, and do the protocols satisfy these?
  - What methods are required to receive alerts and query building?
  - Agree on basic message elements that need to be supported.
  - Agreement on extending CAP to allow event filtering.
- Thursday morning: Security and Standard Access Point (SAP)
  - Discussion of security requirements and approaches to addressing security
  - Agree on principle and outline of SAP
- How do we move forward? Identification of stakeholders and leaders to coordinate.

Emergency Data eXchange Language – Distribution Element (EDXL-DE)

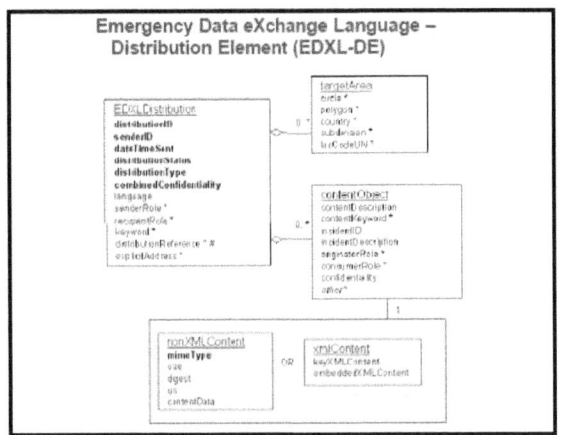

Common Alerting Protocol (CAP)

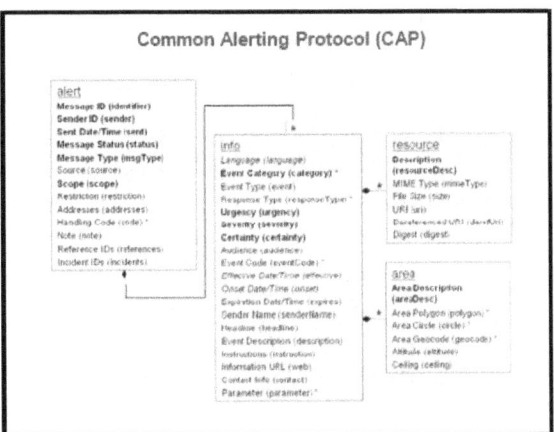

National Information Exchange Model (NIEM)

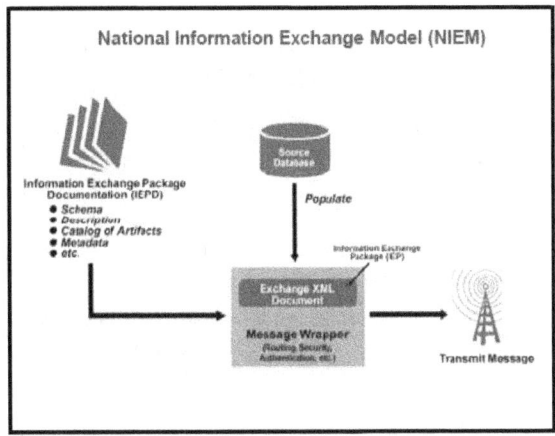

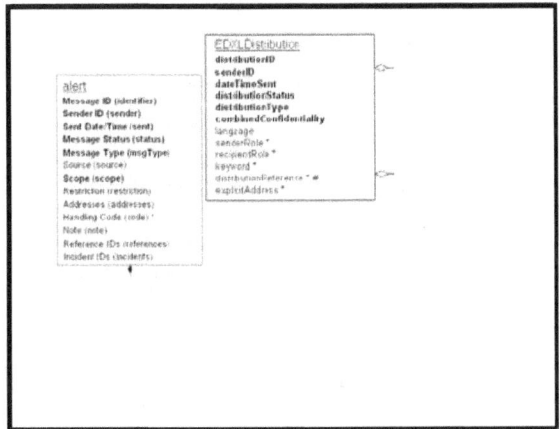

How is Data Interoperability Accomplished?

Technical

- Infrastructure
  - Public - Web
  - Public Safety - Nlets, RISS
- Data Standards
  - GJXDM / NIEM
  - CAP
  - EDXL family of standards

Non-Technical

- Willingness
- Collaboration
- MOU's
- Security Considerations
- Privacy Considerations
- Governance

Why data standards for PSAP's?

Operational Perspective:

- COST Effective way to share data
  - Fewer Custom Interfaces
  - Less Manual Intervention
- Technical Support is easier for PSAP
- Vendors have common standards
- Federal Funding driving standards

Relevant National Initiatives

- GJXDM – Global Justice XML Data Model
- NIEM – National Information Exchange Model
- CAP – Common Alerting Protocol
- EDXL – Emergency Data eXchange Language

Global Justice XML Data Model (GJXDM)

- XML based data reference model
- Global IS Initiative/ISWG, XSTF, GTRI
- Sponsored by DOJ/OJP/BJA
- Common language, vocabulary, methodology
- Justice and public safety specific
- National Standard independent of technology
- Widely utilized today – Government/Industry

National Information Exchange Model (NIEM)

- Built upon GJXDM
- Global Information Sharing Initiative
- Sponsored by DOJ, DHS, ODNI
- Embraces technology and application characteristics of GJXDM
  - Common Language, vocabulary, methodology
- Designed to extend the reach of Justice and public safety to all relevant domains
- Release 2.0 now available

Common Alerting Protocol (CAP)

- OASIS/ EMTC
- Sponsored by DHS/FEMA
- Partners include Emergency Interoperability Consortium (Industry)
- Format for exchanging all-hazard emergency alerts and public warnings independent of technology and networks
- Stand-alone protocol and payload for EDXL messages

Emergency Data eXchange Language (EDXL)

- OASIS EMTC
- Sponsored by DHS/FEMA
- XML based application
- Integrated framework designed for broad EM data exchange application
- Provides a standard message distribution framework
- Utilized over all data transport technologies (SOAP HTTP)
- Facilitates routing of XML formatted emergency messages

Why Standards Matter

- Common Language and Understanding
- Coordinated Approach
- Modular Development
- Cost Savings and Reuse
- Support Infrastructure

IEPD Lifecycle

Business Driven Information Exchange

A NIEM IEPD can also be reused in whole or in part to speed development and lower the cost of defining new information exchanges

A NIEM information exchange begins with a business need for sharing information by a Community of Interest (COI) within and across organizational and jurisdictional boundaries

IEPD documents the Information Exchange Package (IEP) that will be implemented to support the information sharing needs for COI's.

The Information Exchange Package Documentation (IEPD) is used to define how an exchange should be expressed using NIEM

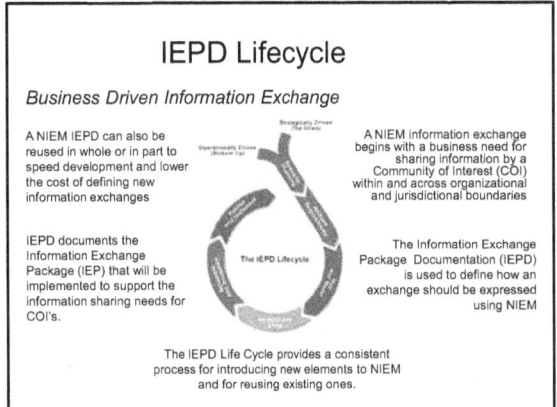

The IEPD Life Cycle provides a consistent process for introducing new elements to NIEM and for reusing existing ones.

IPSTSC CAD IEPD Project

- CAD to CAD IEPD's
  - Initial CFS Transfer
  - Query resource availability
  - Respond to resource availability
  - Subscribe to Unit Update
  - Unit Updates
  - Request Resource
  - Respond to resource request
  - CAD to RMS
- Some Additional IEPD definition efforts:
  - Extension to Fire and EMS
  - External Alerts & Request for Service
  - CAD to RMS (transfers and queries)
  - RMS to RMS
  - Victim Notification
  - Prescription Drugs

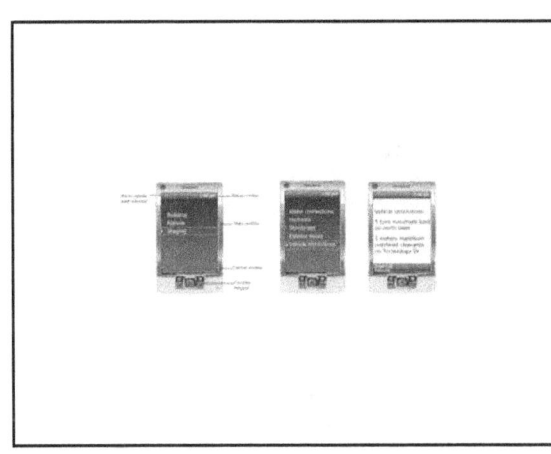

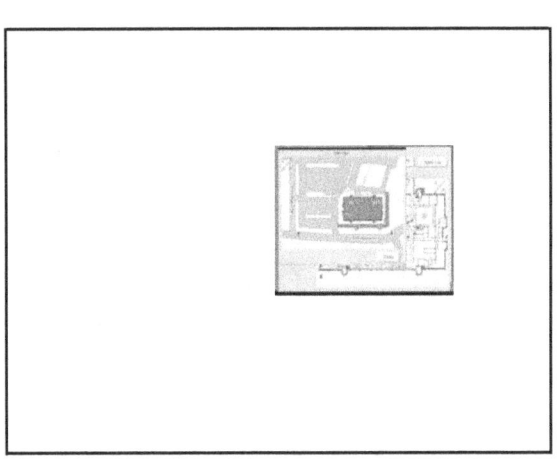

Slide 1 (top left):

- The name and address of the destination and nearest intersection
- A short summary description of the first alarm event including: time of event; location of first event (e.g. loor and room or quadrant); type of alarm in tiation (e.g. manual pu l-stat on, smoke, heat, chem cal, report from individua). For example: 12:01AM Floor 11 Room 11 37 Wa er owing
- A graphical display of the bui ding showing its entire ootprint and the adjacent streets with street names.
- A graphical display of the ocation of the ire or medical emergency on the footprint of the bu ding providing its approximate p an view ocation.
- The detected ex ent of the fire or other event including additional alarms
- A graphical display showing the approxima e locat on of building features including:
  - Standpipes
  - Fire ighter connect ons
  - Hazardous materials
  - Fire ighter e evators
  - Exterior doors and normal state—locked or unlocked
  - Hazardous structures
  - Security guard loca ion
  - Emergency responder display location
  - Hydrants
  - Fire depa tment connections w th sprink er or standpipe designa ion
  - Fire key box (Knox box)
  - Stairways including des gnation of stairs accessing the oof
  - E evators with range of loor designat on
  - Areas of refuge
  - S gnificant hazards associated with the building or bui ding s te
  - Fire truck we ght limits, height or width constraints
  - Compass directions
  - Capabi ity to rota e the building footprint to match where the emergency vehic e s parked.
  - Capabi ity to zoom in and out of the footprint.
  - Pr ority of routing of fire services

Slide 2 (top right):

- An interactive control that a lows the user to select the en route display, initial assessment, or command display.
- Capabi ity to add customized icons.
- Areas served in the building by each fire department connection.
- Building side labels – A, B, C, D
- Sprinkler status – flowing or trouble.
- Operating status of each elevator
  - a. E evator in normal operat on.
  - b. E evator ava lable or occupant evacuation.
  - c. Elevator operating under fire department control.
  - d. E evator out of service.
- Potential collapse warning.
- Location and type of responding apparatus currently at the scene.
- Capabi ity to highlight
- Display of
  - a. Temperature
  - b. Carbon dioxide leve s at the sensor locat on
  - c. Video
  - d. Combinat on of sensor information within a zone
- Triage areas
- Recommended route to the destination
- Obstructions en route
- Areas in the building that are served by each fire department connection
- Fire floor access

Slide 3 (bottom left):

Disp ay o the locat on o the i e on a g aph cal (o examp a oo plan) v ew o the bui ding
High ligh ing o the i at ata m and most recent a e m by a spec al ndicat on such as lashing o animat on
An inte ac ive cont ol to navigate between loo s o the building shown on he g aphical display and to select he oo o inte est o display
An inte ac ive cont ol to navigate is ound a single oo o a la ge o wide bui ding on the g aphical display
Disp ay o the locat on o bui ding eatu es ncluat o i e ghting on the g aph cal view o the bui ding ncluding

- Standpipes
- Hydrants
- Firewal s
- Hazardous materials
- Gas shutoffs
- Power shutoffs
- HVAC shutoffs
- Master sprinkler shutoff
- Own ocation (locat on of the Fixed Location Display)
- Elevators
- Stairs
- Exits
- Locked doors
- Points of access to the roof
- Fire phones
- Fire keybox (Knox box)
- Pre-pos tioned firefighting gear
- Airpack refi ling s ations
- Halon fire suppression systems
- Fuel and compressed gas tanks

Compass d ect ons labe ed clea ly
On he g aphical d splay o he oo -level o the building d splay the ol owing in o ma ion

  - a. Roof access doo s and their condit on-locked or not ocked
  - b. Hazardous construc ion features such as steel bar joists or ens oned concre e. A sample annotation m ght be HAZARD: TENSIONED CONCRETE
  - c. Heavy objects such as coo ing towers, generators, or air hand ers
  - d. Ai/smoke evacuat on ven s or ducts

G aph cal display o a bu lding s te plan that shows the immed ate s te su ounting he building and ncludes he ol owing eatu es access at exits oads d veways pa k ing o a emer gency access pathways such as s dewalks g eway a eas su iciently wide and l m to accommodate a l e igh ing vehicles bui d ng ent ances standpipes and p ima y and seconda y hyd an s a ge vo um hyd ants shall be d s ingu shed om a single d hyd ants

Slide 4 (bottom right): (blank)

NG9-1-1, CSAN, ECC and BISACS Functional View

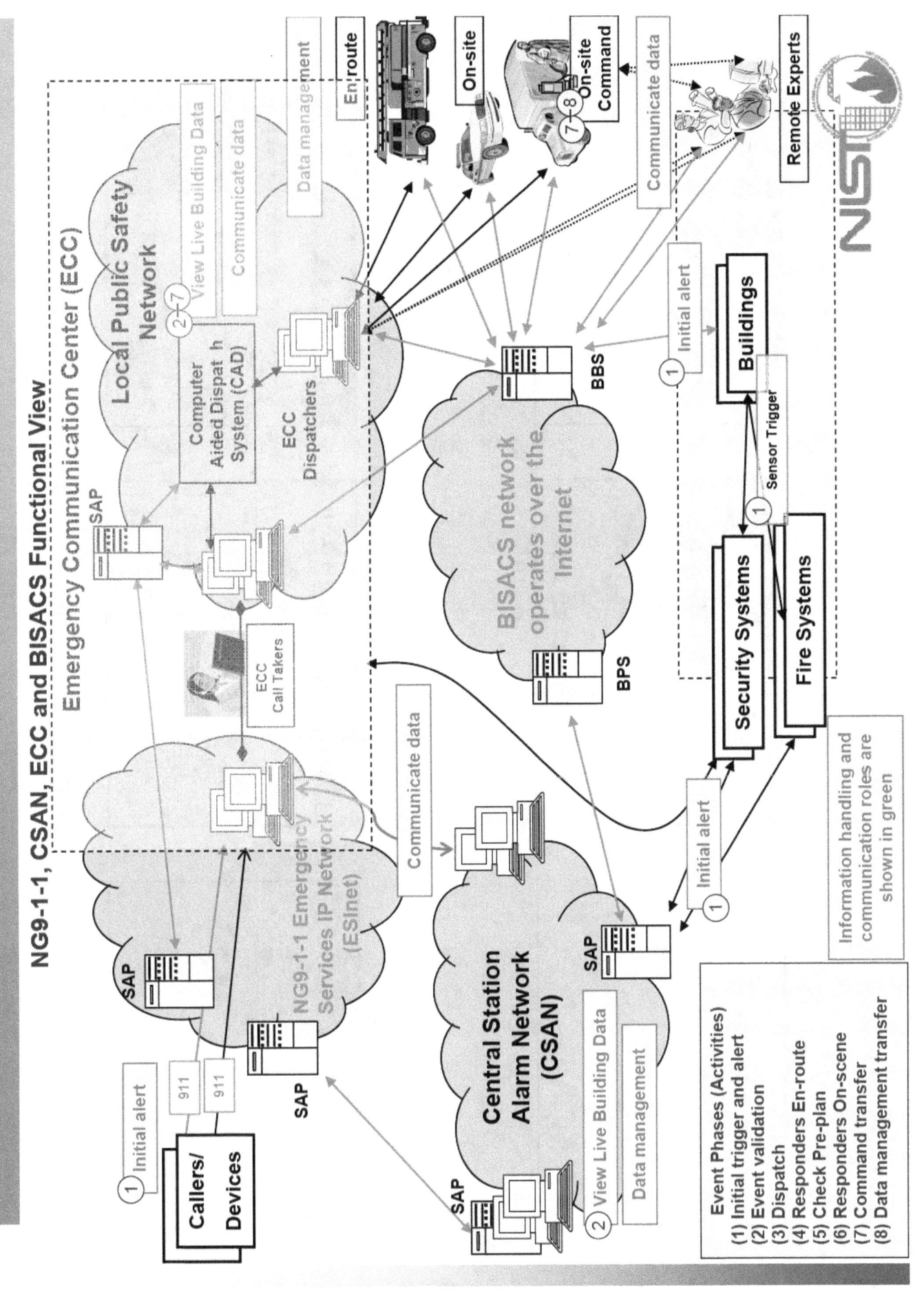

What is NIEM?

- *Data Dictionary* of agreed-to Terms and Definitions
- *Object Oriented Data Model* providing components for creating Information Exchange Packages (IEP)
- *Set of Specifications* for building NIEM components and IEPs
- Governance processes and support infrastructure
- *Clearinghouse* of reusable IEP Documentation (IEPD)
- *Online Web-based Tools* for building IEPDs
- *Training, Knowledge Center,* and *Helpdesk*
- *Technical Assistance* for NIEM Domains and IEPD development
- *Program* providing NIEM leadership and Management *Stakeholder*
- *Operational practitioner driven* Model and Program
- *Partnership* of local, state, tribal, and federal entities

Scenario Based Planning

- Building Collapse: The result of....
  - Terrorist Incident
  - Natural Disaster
  - Large Scale Criminal Event
  - Catastrophic Structural Failure
- Will trigger a broad range of information exchanges across many domains:
  - Law Enforcement
  - Fire Services
  - Emergency Medical Services
  - Disaster Management
  - Environmental
  - Public Works
  - Private Industry
  - Etc.

Information sharing is a national imperative

In detecting, preventing, responding to and investigating crimes, disasters and terrorist acts, the exchange of information among multiple engaged agencies must be *timely and accurate* and therefore highly *automated*.

Most existing computer systems are not designed to facilitate information sharing *across disciplines* and jurisdictions.

Automated information sharing *between agencies* requires the definition of common *standards* for linking disparate systems among federal, state, local and tribal agencies.

Glimpse Into NIEM at 5000 Feet

NIEM Data Dictionary

NIEM Schema XML View

NIEM Reference Schema

NIEM Overview

NIEM at 50,000 Feet

There are Currently seven NIEM Domains

NIEM Core
- People (Person, Organization)
- Places (Location)
- Things (Property, Contact Info, MetaData)
- Events (Activity)

Domains: Infrastructure Protection, Immigration, Intelligence, Person Screening, Justice, Emergency Management, International Trade

Examples of Federal Adoption and Use

- DOJ and DHS have both adopted NIEM
  - DHS has over 45 NIEM IEPDs completed or in development
- The Program Manager - Information Sharing Environment (PM-ISE) designated NIEM as the ISE data partition standard
- The FBI Criminal Justice Information Services (CJIS) Advisory Policy Board (APB) voted to migrate the exchanges supported by the National Crime Information Center (NCIC) to NIEM
- FBI has released the preliminary IEPD and schema for N-DEx consistent with release 2.0 of NIEM and release 3.0 of LEXS (Law Enforcement Information Sharing Program (LEISP) Exchange Specification that includes a family of reusable NIEM-conformant components)
- The recently-released Suspicious Activity Report IEPD focuses on counter-terrorism information sharing

NIEM State and Local Adoption and Use

- Majority of states are engaging NIEM through pilot projects and operational developments
- A few examples:
  - California Administrative Office of the Courts project to develop and publish a library of NIEM IEPD's
  - Florida Law Enforcement eXchan_e FLEX_s stem includes develo_ment of a NIEM compliant data model and IEPDs
  - New York Division of Criminal Justice Services utilizing NIEM to implement at CJIS information exchanges – eJustice Portal
  - Pennsylvania's JNET project developing a plan for upgrading GJXDM based information exchanges to NIEM
  - "Texas Path to NIEM" project developing a blueprint for Texas state and local agencies to cooperatively reach NIEM compliance
  - Consortium for the Exchange of Criminal-Justice Technology (CONNECT) multi-state NIEM-based project (AL, KS, NB, TN WY)
  - Recently released State and Local Suspicious Activity Report IEPD

Identify Information Exchanges

The scenario describes in narrative form an operational situation, business context, legislative, judicial or executive mandate, or other circumstance which must be addressed. From this scenario individual, discrete information exchanges are identified for subsequent analysis and IEPD development.

NIEM References and Links

- NIEM Public Website
  - www.niem.gov
  - Subscribe to NIEM News
  - E-mail information@niem.gov
- National Information Sharing Standards (NISS) Helpdesk and Knowledge Center
  - www.it.ojp.gov/NISShelpdesk
  - E-mail nisshelp@ijis.org
  - Call 1-877-333-5111 or 1-703-726-1919, 9AM-8PM (EST)
- GJXDM/NIEM IEPD Clearinghouse
  - www.it.ojp.gov/iepd/

Summary

- NIEM: Enabler for Information Interoperability and Sharing
  - Responsive to operational information sharing priority needs
  - Practitioner driven at local, state, tribal, and federal levels
  - Solid business and technical foundational components
  - Fit within enterprise information sharing architecture
  - Ensure security and privacy rights are protected
  - Well managed, governed, and supported
  - Broad adoption and use
  - Reuse at all levels

Why NIEM Now?

1. NIEM Is Tested, Ready, and in Production.
2. Documentation and Tools Are Available.
3. Training and Technical Assistance Are Available.
4. A Release Plan Is in Place.
5. Future Grants Will Mandate N EM Conformance.
6. Reference IEPDs Are Being Developed.
7. NIEM Is the Means for Intergovernmental Information Sharing.

National Emergency
Communications Plan (NECP)

DHS, July 2008

- **Recommended National Milestones:**
  - Within 24 months, develop standards for the exchange of real-time situational information for emergency responders before, during, and after an incident.
  - Within 36 months, develop voluntary consensus standards for emergency communications data file structures and messaging formats.

National Emergency
Communications Plan (NECP)

DHS, July 2008

- **Initiative 4.1: Adopt voluntary consensus standards for voice and data emergency response capabilities.**
  - Voluntary consensus standards will enable agencies to make informed procurement decisions and to benefit from emerging technologies. Compliance assessment programs provide a documented certification process for communications equipment and programs.

National Emergency Communications Plan & EM Domain Refresh

NIEM's Emergency Management Domain Refresh

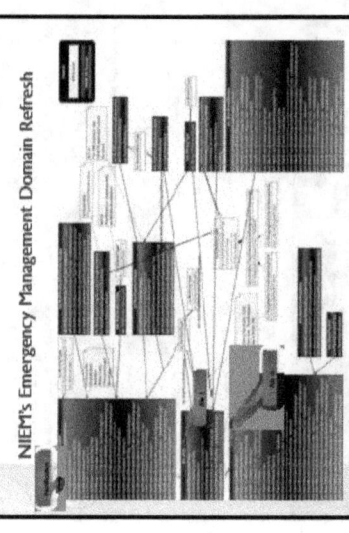

NIEM Domain Refresh:

Emergency Management

Description: The data describes notification information, including alert and alarm information. The data elements and attributes were modeled from existing Emergency Data eXchange Language (EDXL) message standards: Common Alert Protocol (CAP v1.1) and Distribution Element (DE). These elements were vetted against NIEM Core and altered to meet the NIEM Naming and Design Rules (NDR).

- Statistics:
  - Number of Elements: 127
  - Number of Types 28

- **Changes to Existing Material:** All existing material (except for 'Alarm') was removed and replaced with new content based on EDXL

- **Next Step:** Formalize Domain Stewardship.

Executive Summary

External Alarm Interface Exchange

By Bill Hobgood,
DIT Public Safety Team Project Manager &
Interim Applications Solutions Division Manager

National Information Exchange Model (NIEM) at 50,000 Feet

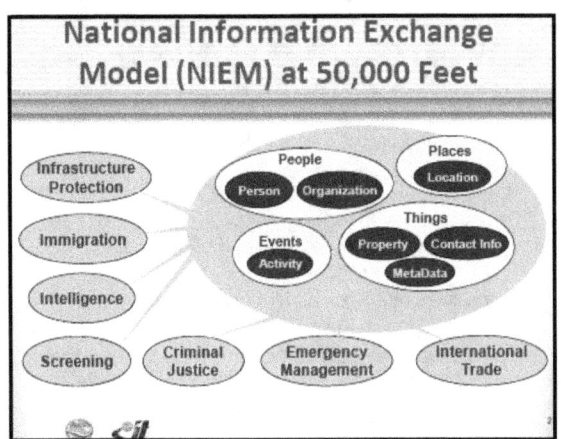

What NIEM Is

- A **National Standard** that facilitates information sharing:
  - ◆ Across organizational and jurisdictional boundaries
  - ◆ At all levels of government
- A **Data Model** providing:
  - ◆ Agreed-upon terms, definitions, and formats for various business concepts
  - ◆ Agreed-upon rules for how those concepts fit together
  - • Independence from how information is stored in individual agency systems
- A **Structured Approach** for:
  - ◆ Development tools, processes, and methodologies

What NIEM is Not

- A database schema
- Just a data dictionary
- Only applicable to the Federal government
  - ◆ Includes many other communities at all levels of government
- A programming language
- A replacement for interagency agreements
  - ◆ NIEM is the technical solution, the policy and business issues must also be worked out

NIEM Participating Communities

What Does NIEM Address?

- The question of "how"
- Improves public safety and homeland security.
- Enhances the quality of justice and decision-making.
- Improves efficiency and effectiveness.
- Facilitates business transformation.
- Achieves greater efficiency, effectiveness, and return on investment (ROI) in operations and decision-making.

What Does NIEM Address? (2 of 2)

- Improves public safety and homeland security.
- Enhances the quality of justice and decision-making.
- Achieves greater efficiency, effectiveness, and return on investment (ROI) in operations and decision-making.
- Improves efficiency and effectiveness.
- Facilitates business transformation.
- Provides a valuable framework, infrastructure and governance that is scalable beyond the current domains for other cross-government information exchange challenges.

What is an IEPD?

- Information Exchange Package Documentation
  - Provides the information exchange specification
  - Includes business artifacts (process, context)
    - Interagency agreements, ConOps, business case, etc.
  - Includes technical artifacts (structure, scope)
    - Schemas, UML, stylesheets, sample XML instances, etc.

What is an IEP?

- Information Exchange Package
  - An XML instance conforming to the IEPD specification
  - Contains the transaction or message-level data passed between two information systems
  - The payload.....

NIEM Example #1

Vehicle Make

- NCIC: Vehicle Make = Message Key VMA
             Example: VMA/FORD

- FBI: <VMACodeType>
             Example: <VMACodeType>FORD</VMACodeType>

- NIEM Core: <VehicleMakeCode>
             Example: <VehicleMakeCode>FORD</VehicleMakeCode>

NIEM Example #2

Vehicle Color

- NCIC: Vehicle Color = Message Key VCO
             Example: VCO:BLK/WHI

- FBI: <VCOCodeType>
             Example: <VCOCodeType>BLK/WHI</VCOCodeType>

- NIEM Core: <VehicleColorPrimaryCode>
             <VehicleColorSecondaryCode>
             <VehicleColorInteriorText>
    Examples: <VehicleColorPrimaryCode>WHI</VehicleColorPrimaryCode>
             <VehicleColorSecondaryCode>BLK</VehicleColorSecondaryCode>
             <VehicleColorInteriorText>GREEN</VehicleColorInteriorText>

A Case Study

APCO – CSAA
External Alarm Interface Exchange

External Alarm Interface Exchange

Purpose
To provide a standard data exchange for electronically transmitting information between an Alarm Monitoring Company and a Public Safety Answering Point (PSAP).

External Alarm Interface Exchange

Background / History
- August, 2004: The Association of Public Safety Communications Officials (APCO) and the Central Station Alarm Association (CSAA) solicit participants as a work group to create and test a data exchange between a CSAA member company and a 911 PSAP. The first beta PSAP chosen is York County, Virginia, and Vector Security is selected as the CSAA member participant. York County is using a copy of Richmond's CAD System installed in 1986.

- October, 2004: First data template is completed.

External Alarm Interface Exchange

Background / History (continued)
- January, 2005: APCO and the CSAA formerly announce a partnership to develop an exchange that will be consistently used by CAD providers and Central Station Alarm Companies for PSAPs to increase efficiency and decrease errors.

- July 22, 2006: The Alarm Interface Exchange 2.0 goes live at York County but includes only Burglar and Hold-up alarms.

External Alarm Interface Exchange

Background / History (continued)
- August 4, 2006: The City of Richmond is requested by APCO to join the pilot test to generate additional volumes of alarm exchanges & goes live.

- October 24, 2006: The alarm exchange has been so successful that all stakeholders agree to expand the pilot to include Fire and Medical alarms.

- September 11, 2007: The City of Richmond implements the new Intergraph CAD System. The alarm interface continues using InterCAD.

External Alarm Interface Exchange

Background / History (continued)
- January, 2008: A Steering Committee is formed for the new Public Safety Data Interoperability (PSDI) project. Funding is provided by the DOJ through the Edward Byrne grant. The project will be managed jointly by APCO and IJIS.

- April 2 – 3, 2008: The PSDI steering committee meets face to face at APCO HQs and identifies possible candidate exchanges with CAD Systems. The External Alarm Interface Exchange is selected as the committee's highest priority for IEPD development.

External Alarm Interface Exchange

Background / History (continued)
- June 17, 2008: IJIS issues an RFP for the development of the alarm exchange IEPD.

- July 9, 2008: IJIS awards IEPD contract to Waterhole software.

- August 27, 2008: IEPD is completed.

- September 9, 2008: IEPD is published on NIEM.GOV's web site.

External Alarm Interface Exchange

Background / History (continued)

- September 12, 2008: External Alarm Interface Exchange is submitted to the APCO ANS process as a recommended standard.

External Alarm Interface Exchange

Three Primary Uses

1. Initial Notification of an Alarm Event by an Alarm Monitoring Company to the PSAP

2. Bi-directional update of status between an alarm monitoring company and the PSAP

3. Bi-directional update of other events between an alarm monitoring company and a PSAP

External Alarm Interface Exchange

Three Primary Benefit Goals

1. Elimination of the telephone call from the Alarm Monitoring Company to the PSAP.

External Alarm Interface Exchange

Three Primary Benefit Goals

I can't understand you. How do you spell that street? I can't hear you, call back.

2. Elimination of miscommunication between the Alarm Monitoring Company operator and the PSAP's call-taker.

External Alarm Interface Exchange

Three Primary Benefit Goals

3. A decrease in response times to alarm-related calls-for-service with an increase in law enforcement apprehensions made, fires more quickly extinguished, and lives saved.

External Alarm Interface Exchange

Three Primary Benefit Goals
1. Elimination of the telephone call from the Alarm Monitoring Company to the PSAP.

2. Elimination of miscommunication between the Alarm Monitoring Company operator and the PSAP's call-taker.

3. A decrease in response times to alarm-related calls-for-service with an increase in law enforcement apprehensions made, fires more quickly extinguished, and lives saved.

External Alarm Interface Exchange

Primary Benefit Outcomes
1. More than 5,000 alarm exchanges have been transmitted to the two Virginia PSAPs without the need of a telephone call from the alarm company and without need of call-taker involvement.
2. Spelling mistakes have been eliminated. No low volume headset issues. No more need to try to interpret foreign accents.
3. The traditional average call-taker processing time to receive and enter an alarm CFS without any repetition is one minute. Some alarm calls take 2 ½ - 3 minutes or more to process. The average turnaround time via the interface is 15 seconds.

External Alarm Interface Exchange

Good Examples of Some Really Bad Alarm Calls

Bad Call #1

External Alarm Interface Exchange

Good Examples of Some Really Bad Alarm Calls

Bad Call #2

External Alarm Interface Exchange

Good Examples of Some Really Bad Alarm Calls

Bad Call #3

External Alarm Interface Exchange

Implementation Recommendations & Assumptions
1. Alarm Companies will continue to follow SOP concerning contact attempts with someone on the premise prior to sending the call to the PSAP.

2. PSAPs will be in control of filtering alarm response requests, for example mass rejection of all alarm requests when a catastrophic event is occurring.

3. The PSAP will continue to take responsibility to identify high-risk or target locations, and not the alarm company.

External Alarm Interface Exchange

Implementation Recommendations (continued)
4. NENA standards will be utilized for addressing purposes.

5. Each _ artici_ atin_ Alarm Monitorin_ Com_ an_ will assign a liaison to coordinate new implementations both internally and externally with the PSAP and the alarm company's software provider. PSAPs will likewise assign a liaison to work with the alarm company and the CAD provider.

6. First Responder deployment and response plans are strictly business decisions of the PSAP.

External Alarm Interface Exchange

Implementation Recommendations (continued)
7. Prior to the live cutover of any interface, the address of all alarm subscribers should be sent to the PSAP / CAD by the Alarm Company in bulk to identify address that have issues and cannot be validated.
8. Upon the creation of a new account, the Alarm Company will transmit an address validation request to the PSAP / CAD to ensure that the address will geo-validate.
9. Alarm Companies will have a procedure in place to call the PSAP if no acknowledgement is received within "x" seconds following an alarm transmission.

External Alarm Interface Exchange

Implementation Recommendations (continued)
10. Alarm Companies should include geo-coordinates for each address in the exchange

11. CAD providers should geo-validate in this order:
   - By street address (if present)
   - By geo-coordinates if geo-coordinates are present, and if no street address is present or if the street address cannot be validated
   - By intersection if two cross-streets are provided, and if no street address is present and no geo-coordinates are present. This is a rare situation.

External Alarm Interface Exchange

Implementation Recommendations (continued)
12. The PSAP and the alarm monitoring company will decide on the event types that will be transmitted. A standard list of event types is provided in the IEPD.

13. The PSAP will work with the CAD system provider to decide how each data element sent by the alarm company will be mapped to the call-for-service record.

14. When Rejecting a new alarm, the response message must include the reason for the rejection.

External Alarm Interface Exchange

Implementation Recommendations (continued)
15. Once the initial new alarm record is sent by the Alarm Monitoring Company, all subsequent Update transmissions to the PSAP must utilize the element name <StatusDescriptionText>. Most PSAPs do NOT want certain fields updated automatically by an external source such as an update to the address.

External Alarm Interface Exchange

For More Information About the IEPD
http://niem.gtri.gatech.edu/niemtools/iepdt/display/conta
iner.iepd?ref=Ow8gz1PI7b4%3D

External Alarm Interface Exchange

Next Steps
- Meeting with NIST mid-October
- Presenting at Virginia APCO/NENA Fall Conference
- Paper Submitted for APCO/NENA 2009 Winter Summit
- Paper Submitted for APCO 2009 Conference
- External Alarm Interface Exchange becomes a National Standard at Some Point During This Period

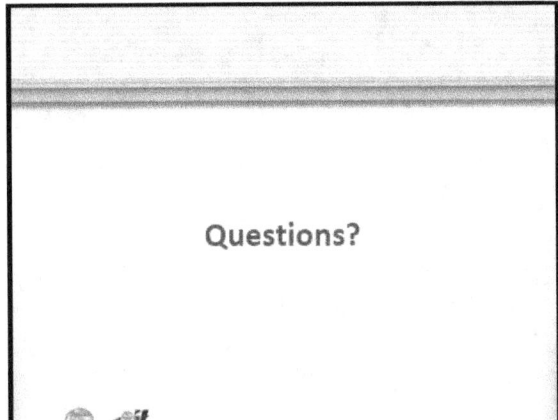

NENA NG9-1-1 – Moving 9-1-1 to IP

Brian Rosen

NEUSTAR

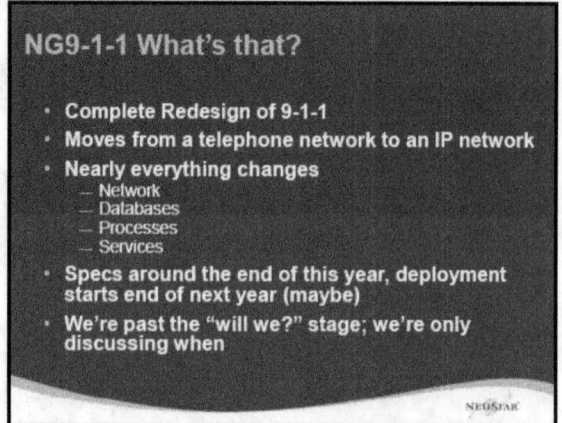

NG9-1-1 What's that?

- **Complete Redesign of 9-1-1**
- **Moves from a telephone network to an IP network**
- **Nearly everything changes**
  - Network
  - Databases
  - Processes
  - Services
- **Specs around the end of this year, deployment starts end of next year (maybe)**
- **We're past the "will we?" stage; we're only discussing when**

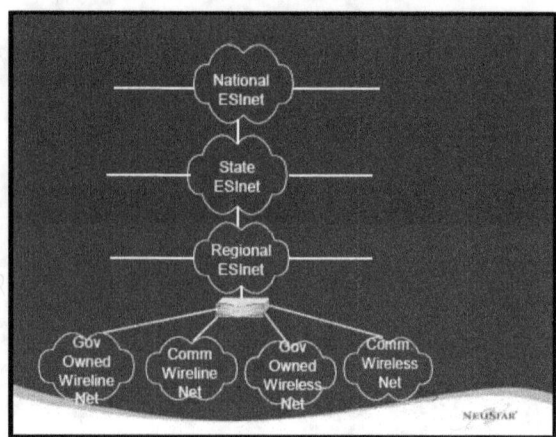

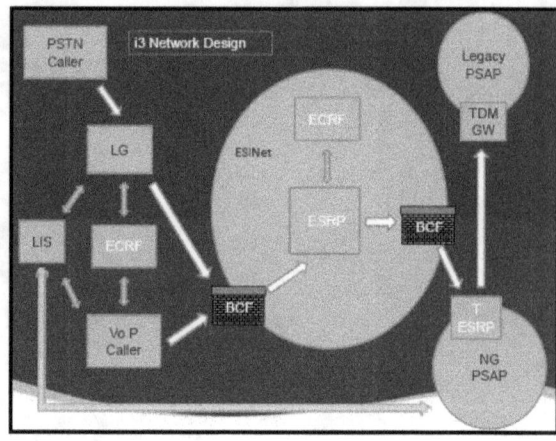

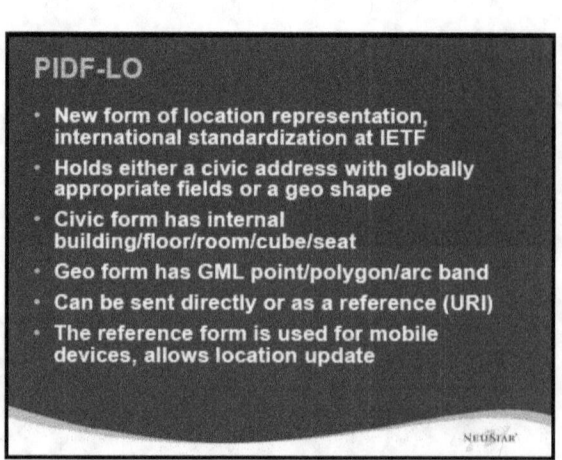

Location Information Server

- **Repository of location information for endpoints**
- **Operated by Access Network**
- **Uses some kind of key to identify the device**
  - MAC address (Ethernet device D)
  - IP address
  - Telephone Number (legacy wireline)
  - ESRK (legacy wireless, with MPC)
- **Returns new form of location, either as a value (geo or civic) or reference (key) – PIDF-LO**
- **Typically, the endpoint gets its own location, but if access network and calling network have a relationship, calling network can add location**

PIDF-LO

- **New form of location representation, international standardization at IETF**
- **Holds either a civic address with globally appropriate fields or a geo shape**
- **Civic form has internal building/floor/room/cube/seat**
- **Geo form has GML point/polygon/arc band**
- **Can be sent directly or as a reference (URI)**
- **The reference form is used for mobile devices, allows location update**

1

Emergency Call Routing Function

- Controls routing of calls within the ESInet
- It's a map (GIS system)
- LoST protocol: Queried with address and "service", returns address of where call should go next
- Used by
  - Devices/calling networks to get call to the right ESInet
  - ESRP within the ESInet to get to the next ESRP or PSAP
  - PSAP to get to responders
- Civic address routing, in theory, is reverse geocode and point-in-polygon
- Can change the routing polygon on the fly if needed (disaster routes)
- All calls are routed by the ECRF, no exceptions
- Provided by 9-1-1 Authority, but can be aggregated or distributed to form a county/state/nation/global route db

NEUSTAR

Border Control Function

- Basic security function for ESInet
- Firewall + "Session Border Controller"
- At least one at entrance to ESInet
- Probabl state level due to bandwidth costs
- Also probably another BCF at entrance to PSAP (trust but verify)
- Operates on PSAP policy for what to admit
- Has PSAP state (normal/under attack) to adjust filtering of calls

NEUSTAR

Emergency Services Routing Proxy

- Call Routing Element of ESInet
- Replaces Selective Router (9-1-1 TDM Switch)
- Uses the ECRF to select a candidate route
- Has extensive Policy Routing Function to control routing
- Receives PSAP state (normal, congested, disaster, under attack, failed)
- Can route calls to any willing PSAP
  - PSAP management always in control of how their calls are handled and who can send them calls

NEUSTAR

All Calls are SIP

- EVERY call entering an ESInet is SIP signaled
- Gateways outside the net deal with legacy or non native-sip
- Standard SIP signaling
- Has location (new "Geolocation" header) & callback (telephone number)
- Routed by ECRF (LoST protocol)
- 3rd Party Calls (e.g. Central Alarm Service) fully supported

NEUSTAR

Additional Data

- Calls arrive with location and callback
- More data may be available
  - Call
  - Caller
  - Location
- Call Data is provided by device or service provider
  - Signaled with a URI in a "Call-Info" header
- Location data URI retrieved from ECRF
  - LoST query with a specific Service URN
- Caller Data can be included in either Call or Location Data
- The "Location Data" is building data
  - Supplied by Building owner and/or tenant

NEUSTAR

Emergency Events

- A "Call" has a human with media
- An event has no human (and therefore no media)
- Calls are CAP messages signaled with SIP "Message" (like IM)
- They Route the same way as calls
- Location is included
- Building data URI can be included
  - Or can be retrieved from ECRF with location
- NENA will define event types

NEUSTAR

One Slide on Security

- ESInet has controlled access, but is NOT assumed to be a walled garden
- All protocol interactions are protected, usually with TLS/Mutual Authentication
- Uniform notion of security for all services
- Federated PKIs for agencies and agents
  - NENA will contract for a PSAP CA (PCA)
- 2 factor authentication of agents (single signon)
- Role based authorization
- Common policy store/editor/formatting

NEUSTAR

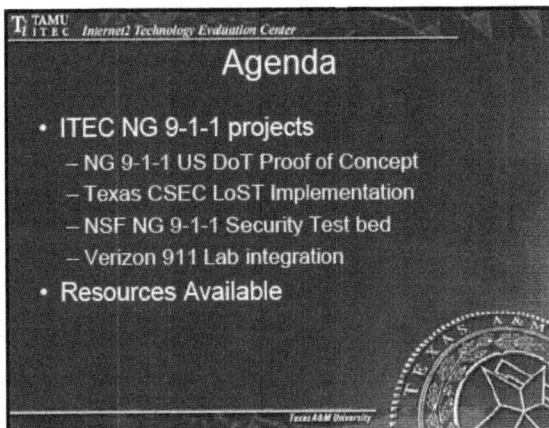

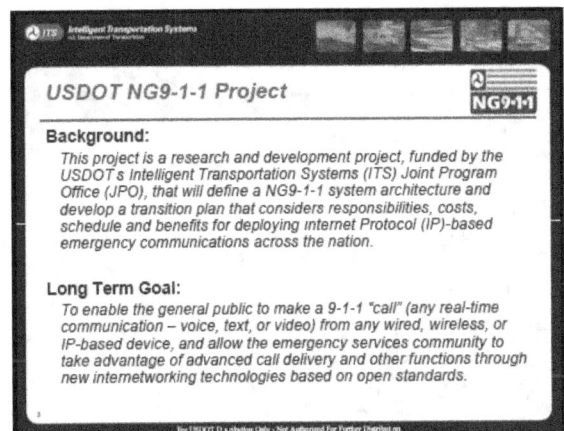

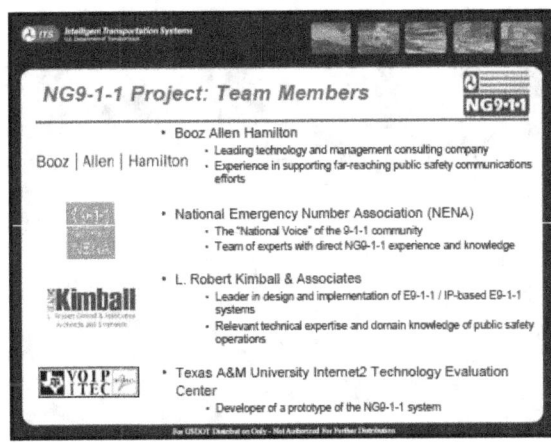

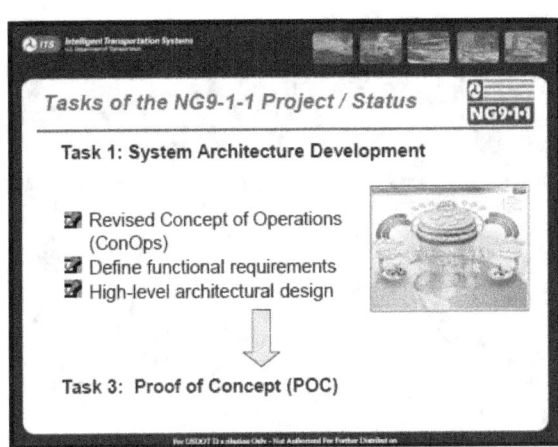

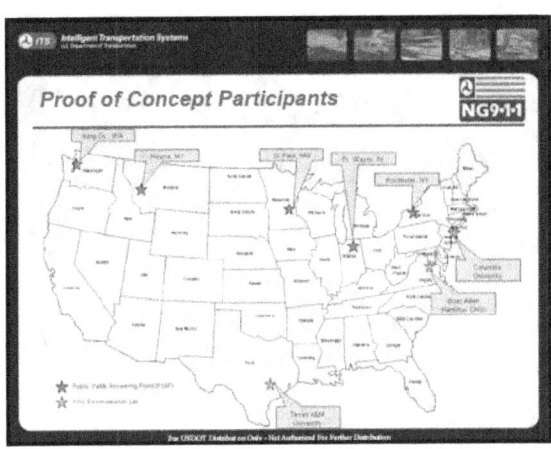

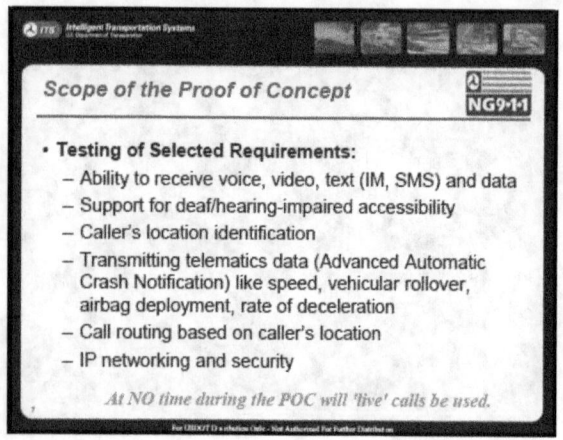

Scope of the Proof of Concept

NG9·1·1

- **Testing of Selected Requirements:**
  - Ability to receive voice, video, text (IM, SMS) and data
  - Support for deaf/hearing-impaired accessibility
  - Caller's location identification
  - Transmitting telematics data (Advanced Automatic Crash Notification) like speed, vehicular rollover, airbag deployment, rate of deceleration
  - Call routing based on caller's location
  - IP networking and security

At NO time during the POC will 'live' calls be used.

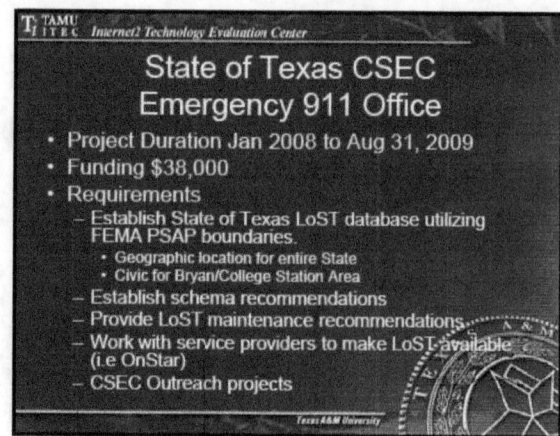

State of Texas CSEC Emergency 911 Office

- Project Duration Jan 2008 to Aug 31, 2009
- Funding $38,000
- Requirements
  - Establish State of Texas LoST database utilizing FEMA PSAP boundaries.
    - Geographic location for entire State
    - Civic for Bryan/College Station Area
  - Establish schema recommendations
  - Provide LoST maintenance recommendations
  - Work with service providers to make LoST available (i.e OnStar)
  - CSEC Outreach projects

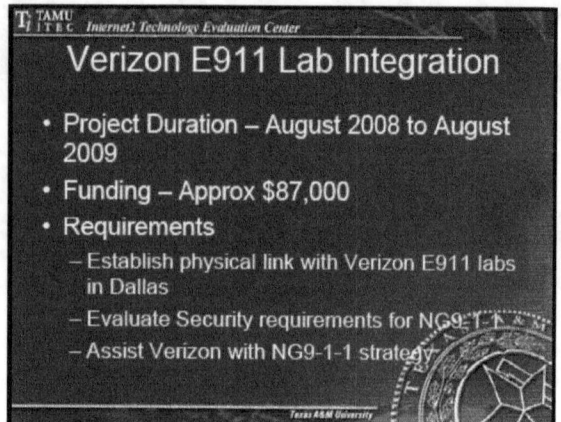

Verizon E911 Lab Integration

- Project Duration – August 2008 to August 2009
- Funding – Approx $87,000
- Requirements
  - Establish physical link with Verizon E911 labs in Dallas
  - Evaluate Security requirements for NG9-1-1
  - Assist Verizon with NG9-1-1 strategy

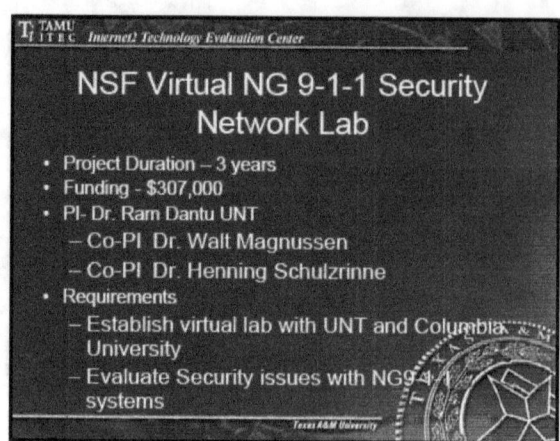

NSF Virtual NG 9-1-1 Security Network Lab

- Project Duration – 3 years
- Funding - $307,000
- PI- Dr. Ram Dantu UNT
  - Co-PI Dr. Walt Magnussen
  - Co-PI Dr. Henning Schulzrinne
- Requirements
  - Establish virtual lab with UNT and Columbia University
  - Evaluate Security issues with NG9-1-1 systems

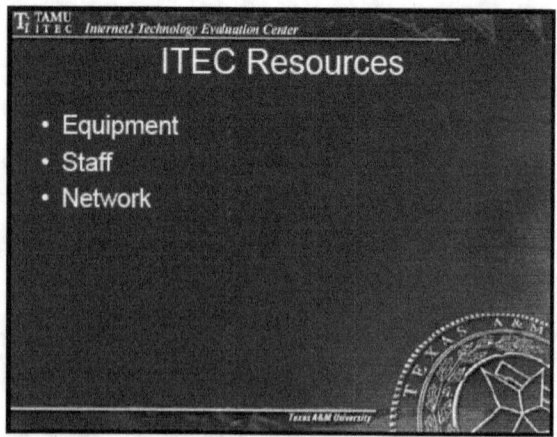

ITEC Resources

- Equipment
- Staff
- Network

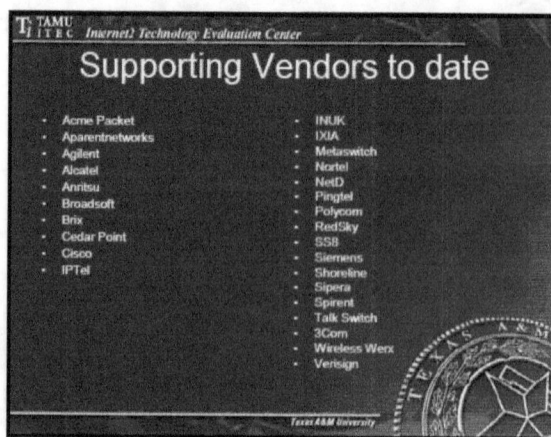

Supporting Vendors to date

- Acme Packet
- Aparentnetworks
- Agilent
- Alcatel
- Anritsu
- Broadsoft
- Brix
- Cedar Point
- Cisco
- IPTel

- INUK
- IXIA
- Metaswitch
- Nortel
- NetD
- Pingtel
- Polycom
- RedSky
- SSB
- Siemens
- Shoreline
- Sipera
- Spirent
- Talk Switch
- 3Com
- Wireless Werx
- Verisign

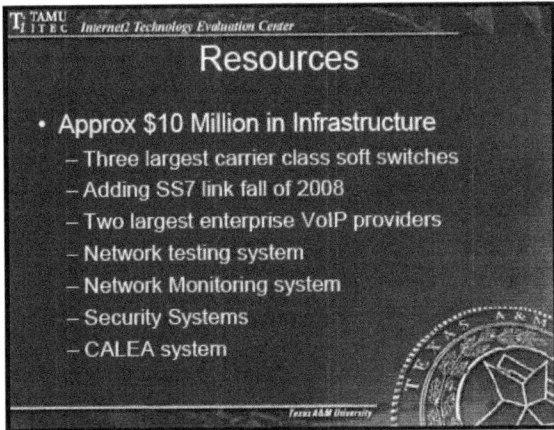

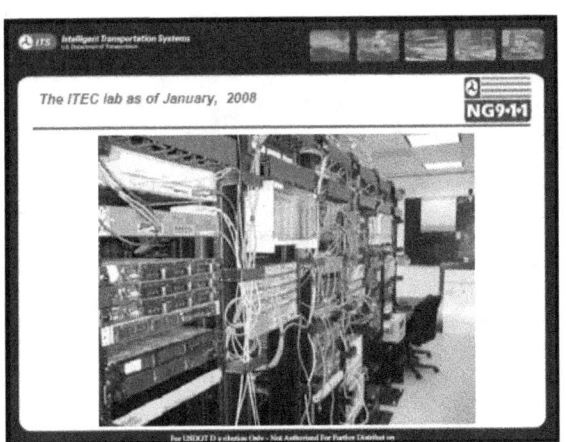

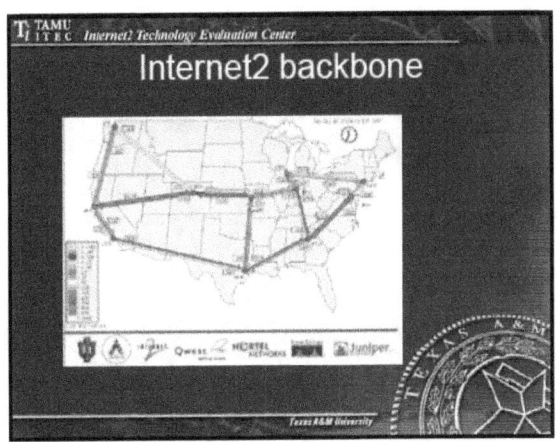

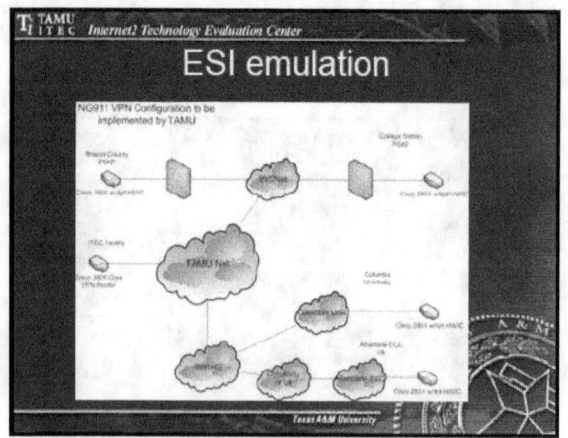

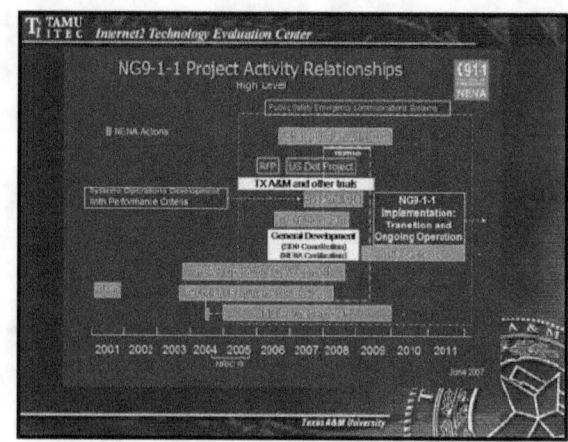

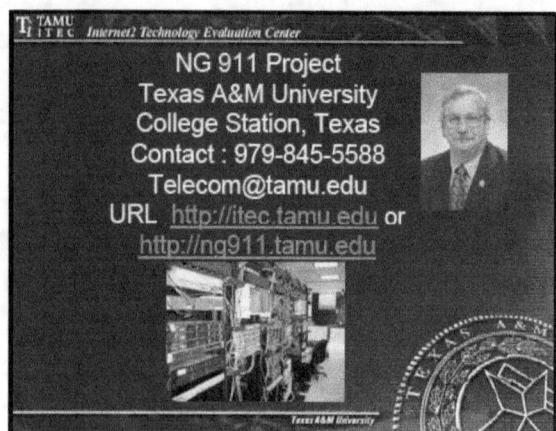

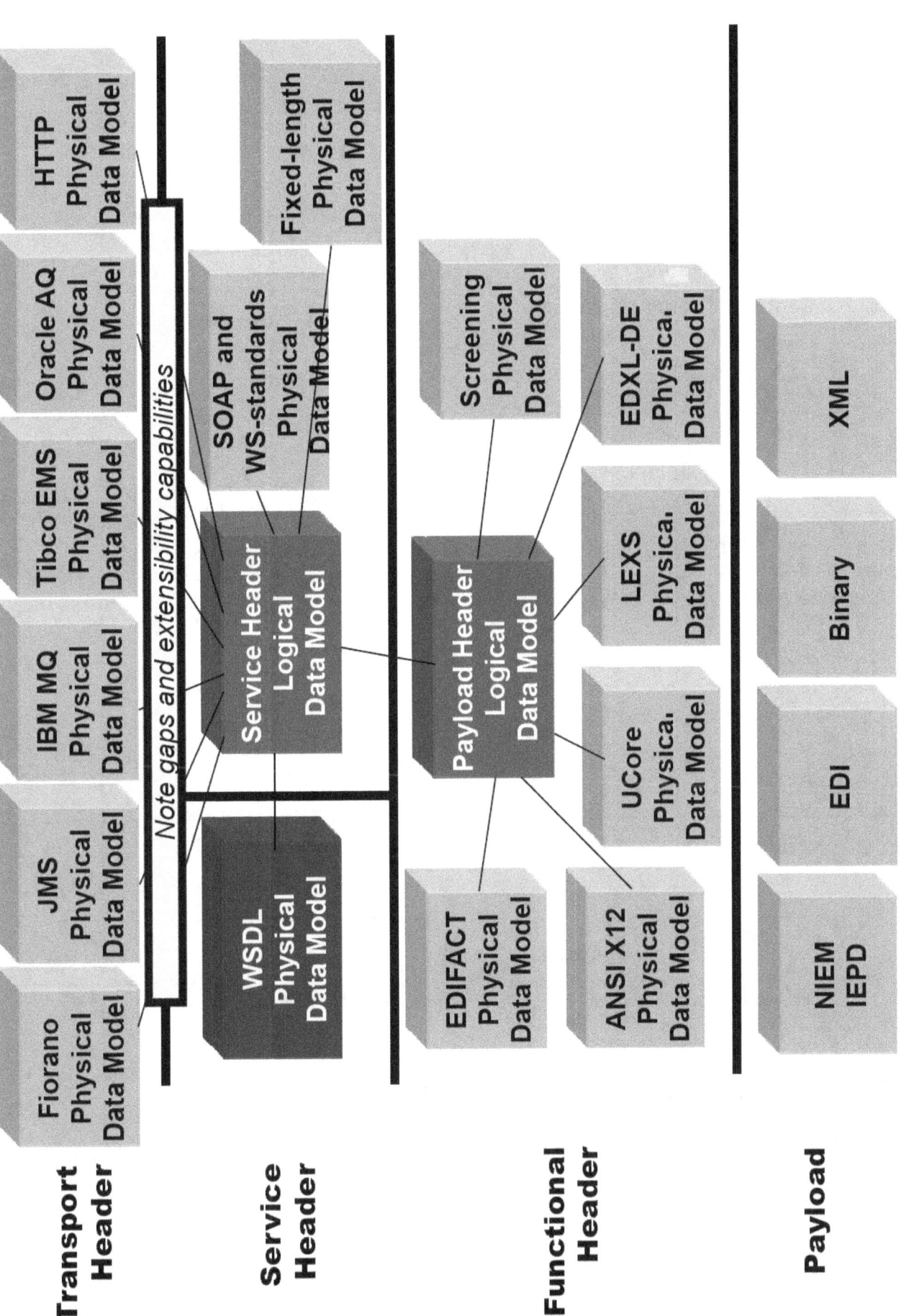

* SB30 Standards / Recommendations

Specified **by the fire service**
for their use
in responding to
fires and other emergencies

* From work within the National Electrical and Manufacturing Association (NEMA) SB30 Task Groups in collaboration with NIST BFRL and First Responders.

Uniform set of requirements

Equipment sufficiently similar across different manufacturers' systems

Results for fire service personnel :

- Display system training has a common framework
- Familiarity with the equipment with a fair degree of confidence

SB30 version 2

- Fire display equipment standards for:
  - Design
  - Operation
  - Arrangement of information
  - Certain control functions
- * addresses portable displays

Current focus (for version 3)

- Communications connectivity
- Security
- Information format

Communication connectivity

- Communication interfaces to connect
  - a remote Fire Service Standard Emergency Interface
  - Building's fire system
- Communication between
  - Building's fire system and
  - Other building systems (elevator, HVAC, security, …)

Security

- Security for user and/or device (authentication and credentialing)
- Policy format for scope level for system interaction (what can be accessed)
  - by whom
  - When
  - from where
- Requirements for securing data
  - during transmission
  - when stored on a remote device

Information format

- Information format for:
  - Information terminology
  - Information structure
  - Data association with other fire critical information
- Common vocabulary and data format for exchange between:
  - Remote devices
  - Building fire systems
- Specifying location based data elements
  - Within the floor plan
  - Within the site plan
  - (In text, audio,   )